BO GEORGE

Complete IN Christ

Discovering God's View of You

HARVEST HOUSE PUBLISHERS
Eugene, Oregon 97402

COMPLETE IN CHRIST

Copyright © 1994 by Harvest House Publishers
Eugene, Oregon 97402

Library of Congress Cataloging-in-Publication Data

George, Bob, 1933–
        Complete in Christ: discovering God's view of you / Bob George.
            p.   cm.
        ISBN 1-56507-203-0
        1. Theology, Doctrinal–Popular works.   I. Title.
    BT77.G42   1994   93-43728
    230—dc20   CIP

Printed in the United States of America.

97   98   99   00   —   10   9   8   7   6   5   4

Contents

1
CHAPTER

The Two
Big Issues

J esus said, "I have come that they may have life, and have it to the full" (John 10:10). Yet many professing Christians today are saying, "There is nothing abundant about my life. I know my sins are forgiven and I am going to heaven, but what about *today*? I still experience doubts, fears, frustrations, and defeat. Surely there must be something more to this Christian life!"

The solution to this dilemma can best be understood through a closer look at Romans 5:10: "If, when we were God's enemies, we were reconciled to Him through the **death** of His Son, how much more, having been reconciled, shall we be saved by His **life!**" The good news of the gospel is not just that Christ came to *die* for you, but that He came to give His *life* to you.

There is no more important fact in the Christian experience than the profound truth that *Christ lives in you*. Misunderstanding this spiritual truth enslaves many Christians to the impossible task of trying to live the Christian life. The inevitable failure of such attempts brings them to the practical conclusion that Christianity does not work.

This lack of emphasis on the living Christ may explain why there is such a great contrast between the church of Jesus Christ today and His church of the first century. In J.B. Phillips' introduction to *Letters to Young Churches* he states:

> The great difference between present-day Christianity and that which we read in these letters [New Testament Epistles] is that to us it is primarily a **performance**; to them, it was a real **experience**. We are apt to reduce the Christian religion to a code or, at best, a rule of heart and life. To these men it is quite plainly the invasion of their lives by a new quality of life altogether. They do not hesitate to describe this as Christ living in them.

Time and time again, as I speak with people on our daily live radio program "People to People," I hear individuals whose lives are torn apart although they are absolutely confident that they are going to heaven when they die. "I accepted Jesus Christ as my Savior when I was 12 years old," they often say. What they mean is "I accepted Christ for what He did for me." However, when I ask if they understand the living Christ Himself **in** them, there is dead silence. In spite of years of failure to experience the abundant life that Jesus provided, these people still declare, "I'll live the Christian life if it kills me!" To this I reply, "You can be sure it will!" Many of us simply have not come to grips with the truth that it is not **hard** to live the Christian life . . . it is impossible!

Jesus said, "You will know the truth, and the truth

will set you free" (John 8:32). If Jesus is God (which He most certainly is), and God said it is truth that sets us free, then it is truth that sets us free! If it is truth that sets us free, what is the only thing that puts us in bondage? The answer is obvious: It is error, lies, or simple ignorance.

The Millionaire
Who Lived in Poverty

A good illustration of the results of a lack of spiritual knowledge is seen in the true story of a west Texas farmer by the name of Yates. Mr. Yates owned a lot of undeveloped land on which he raised sheep, but he lived in poverty. It was during the Depression years, and he was having difficulty even feeding and clothing his family.

As Mr. Yates was facing inevitable bankruptcy, an oil company suddenly approached him and requested permission to drill for oil on his land. Reasoning that he had little to lose, Mr. Yates gave them permission. The oil company began drilling and discovered the largest oil deposit at that time on the North American continent— a deposit which produced 80,000 barrels of oil a day!

At that time oil was selling for about three dollars per barrel. Overnight Mr. Yates became a millionaire. The amazing thing about this incident, though, was that **Mr. Yates had been a millionaire ever since he first signed the papers on the land; he just hadn't known it!**

We are told in 2 Peter 1:3 that "His divine power has given us **everything we need** for life and godliness through our knowledge of Him who has called us by His own glory and goodness." Paul wrote as well, "Praise be to the God and Father of our Lord Jesus Christ, who has blessed us in the heavenly realms with **every spiritual blessing** in Christ" (Ephesians 1:3). The problem with most Christians is that, like Mr. Yates, we are **unaware** of the incredible riches that we **already have** in Christ. In the following pages I would like to share some of the biblical truths that will set you free as you grow in the knowledge of "Christ in you, the hope of glory" (Colossians 1:27).

Salvation Encompasses Two Issues

If I may use an unusual illustration, let us suppose that a man has died of a disease. If you had the power to restore the man, how many problems would you have to cure? The answer is _two_. You would have to raise him to _life_ (the cure for death), but you would also have to deal with the _disease_ that killed him. Look at it this way: Would it make any sense to cure his disease if you couldn't raise him to life? No, you would just have a "healthy dead man" as a result. On the other hand, would it make sense to raise him to life if you could not cure his disease? No, because the disease would only kill him again. You could only truly restore the man by curing _both_ problems.

In the same way, for mankind to be saved spiritually, there were _two issues_ that God had to address: first, man's state of guilt through _sin_ (the disease); second, the _wages_ of sin, man's spiritual state of _death_ (the result of the disease). Unless both of these issues were dealt with, mankind could not be totally saved. To deal with the sin issue alone would leave mankind nothing more than a race of forgiven dead men. On the other hand, to raise people from the dead spiritually without putting away their sins (curing the disease) would doom them to dying again the first time they sinned, for "the wages of sin is death" (Romans 6:23). The result would be what I call "Dracula theology": a person's existence would go back and forth, dead then alive, dead then alive, over and over. Never could he possess what the Bible calls **eternal** life.

It is only as we hold the knowledge of _both_ these issues that the New Testament will make sense to us. As strange as it seems to our ears the first time we hear it, it is biblically true that we are not merely saved by the _death_ of Christ. **We are saved by the resurrected life of Christ!** This is why Romans 5:10 says, "If, when we were God's enemies, we were reconciled to Him through the death of

His Son, how much more, having been reconciled, shall we be saved through His life!" God's solution to the *sin* issue was the cross; His solution to the *life-and-death* issue was the *resurrection* of Jesus Christ.

The Finality of
Christ's Work on the Cross

When we see that the goal of salvation is raising people from the dead and restoring them to a relationship

with God, it becomes obvious that our sins must be taken away **once and for all.** Otherwise, the first time we sinned following our acceptance of Christ, we would die again. The wages of sin always was, always is, and always will be, _death!_ That is, unless we are freed from that law through a higher law. Though the pull of gravity is continual, you can overcome the law of gravity through applying the law of aerodynamics in an airplane. In a similar way, Paul describes our escape from the law of death through taking advantage of a higher spiritual law: "Through Jesus Christ the law of the Spirit of life set me free from the law of sin and death" (Romans 8:2).

Therefore, in order to set us free from the sin issue, here is what the New Testament teaches.

1. Jesus Christ came to take away the sin of the world once and for all. When John the Baptist saw Jesus approaching, He said to his disciples, "Look, the Lamb of God, who takes away the sin of the world!" (John 1:29).

"By [God's] will we have been made holy through the sacrifice of the body of Jesus Christ **once for all.** Day after day every priest stands and performs his religious duties; again and again he offers the same sacrifices, which can never take away sins. But when this priest had offered for all time one sacrifice for sins, He sat down at the right hand of God" (Hebrews 10:10-12).

Under the law, the sin issue could never be put away, "because it is impossible for the blood of bulls and goats to take away sins" (Hebrews 10:4). At best, the animal sacrifices provided an object for the worshiper's faith and a place to transfer his guilt. The sacrifices were, at the time, God's ordained way to _cover_ sins until they could be truly dealt with at some future time. Keep in mind, however, that no Old Testament believer had the blessing of looking back to a completed work. He could receive forgiveness up to date, but the next day his sins began adding up again, demanding another sacrifice.

To make as clear as possible the absolute finality of the work of Jesus Christ on the cross, the writer of Hebrews contrasts the sacrifice of Christ against those continual sacrifices offered by the priests under the Mosaic law. In the first verse of Hebrews 10 he asserts that the rituals of the law were only pictures of the reality that would someday be fulfilled by Christ and His completed work on the cross:

> The law is only a shadow of the good things that are coming—not the realities themselves. For this reason it can never, by the same sacrifices repeated endlessly year after year, make perfect those who draw near to worship.

In contrast to the Old Covenant priests, whose work was never done, we see Jesus Christ *seated* at the Father's right hand. Why is He seated? Because *"It is finished!"* (John 19:30). The sin issue has been dealt with once and for all, and Christ has paid it all! The writer of Hebrews reaches the climax of his argument in 10:14: "Because by one sacrifice He has made perfect forever those who are being made holy." Then, in Hebrews 10:18 is the conclusion: "Where these have been forgiven, there is no longer any sacrifice for sin." Jesus Christ has done it all!

2. As a result of Christ's finished work on the cross, the world has been reconciled to God. "God was reconciling the world to Himself in Christ, not counting men's sins against them. And He has committed to us the message of reconciliation (2 Corinthians 5:19).

Through the work of Jesus Christ on the cross, reconciliation is said to have taken place. Reconciliation means that the cause of man's alienation from God—his sins—has been taken away, and the way has been opened to return to a holy, loving God. Therefore nothing stands between any person and eternal life but his or her own unbelief and rejection of God's gift of salvation through the saving life of Jesus Christ.

The knowledge of Christ's finished work on the cross enables us to put away guilt and have confidence to draw near to God, as well as giving us assurance of our eternal destiny. But this alone is not salvation! It is only half the gospel. The cross was God's way to clear the decks for the divine action of putting Himself back into mankind— that is, the raising of dead people to life.

> This is the testimony: God has given us eternal life, and this life is in His Son. He who has the Son has life; he who does not have the Son of God does not have life. I write these things to you who believe in the name of the Son of God so that you may know that you have eternal life (1 John 5:11-13).

2
CHAPTER

The Nature
of Man

L et's return to the Garden of Eden to get the big picture of what God created man to be, what he became, and what salvation really means. In Genesis 1:27 we are told, "God created man in His own image, in the image of God He created him; male and female He created them." This is a very familiar verse to most people, but I wonder if we stop and think about what it means. The Bible teaches that God is a spirit, without a body or physical form. Therefore Genesis cannot be saying that we physically look like God. What does it mean that man was created in God's image?

Man Has a Body

God created other forms of life, and perhaps we should start there. All living things, whether man, animals, or plants, have one thing in common—a body; that is, a physical form which grows, feeds, breathes, and breeds. You and I have a body, but so do the dogs, cats, insects, and trees. However, in spite of the similarities, there are major differences as well. What separates man and the animal kingdom from the plant kingdom?

Man Has a Soul

Man and the animals have what the Bible calls a **soul**, a behavior mechanism. The simplest definition of a soul

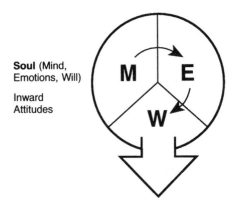

is mind, emotions, and will. It may seem strange at first to think of animals as having souls, but consider a dog. Does a dog have a mind, emotions, and a will? Of course he does, and you can tell what is going on in the dog's soul by watching his body. If he comes up to you directly with tail wagging wildly and his tongue hanging out, you would think, "This dog is safe; he likes me." But if a dog cowers back, tail between his legs, and is making growling noises, you would do well to keep your distance.

The animal kingdom does therefore have a soul—conscious life expressed through intellect, emotions, and will. * The question then must be asked, "In what way, then, is man more than an animal?" The answer is first hinted at in Genesis 2:7, where we are given a more detailed account of man's creation: "The Lord God formed the man from the dust of the ground and breathed into his nostrils the breath of life, and man became a living being." Unlike all other forms of life that God created by mere declaration, He is shown imparting of His own life to man. This is the aspect known as the **spirit**.

Man Has a Spirit

The human spirit is the part of man that enables him to relate to and know God, and is the source of his inner drives for love, acceptance, and meaning and purpose in life. The human spirit was created to be dependent upon and united with God's Spirit, and was the means through which man was intended to enjoy perfect fellowship with God.

The existence of the human spirit explains the differences between man and the animal kingdom. Take a dog as an example again: What does it take to make a dog

---

* Of course it is understood that man has an *eternal* soul while an animal has only a *temporal* soul (a soul until physical death).

happy? You give him a place to sleep, food, water, maybe scratch his back a little, and he is satisfied. Do you ever see him sitting with a thoughtful look on his face asking, "Why am I here? What does all this mean?" Do you see him in depression, pushing his bone aside and

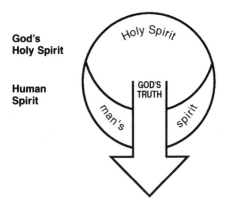

complaining, "There must be more to life than this"? Of course not—that is ridiculous. But there is nothing more human than the asking of these questions. Because we have physical bodies with physical needs there are similarities, but sometime in the life of every human being he begins asking, "Who am I? Why am I here? What is the meaning of life?" That is the working of the human spirit.

Freedom to Choose

Another difference resulting from man's spiritual nature is **free will**. The animal kingdom is governed by an internal programming that we call instinct. Why do the swallows go back year after year on the same date to the same place in San Juan Capistrano? How do the bees in a hive organize themselves to work in such incredible complexity and harmony? How and why do salmon swim hundreds of miles upstream to the very place they were spawned to reproduce and die? We would answer in each case "instinct."

What we mean by instinct is that there is built into the animal kingdom something like a computer program which compels them to act in a certain way. However, it would never occur to you to pat a swallow on the back and say, "Good bird. That was really marvelous. Thank you for your obedience." Why not? Because an animal is not

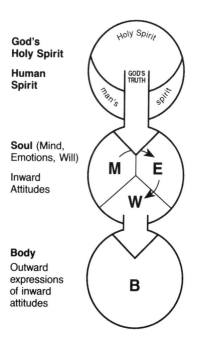

**God's
Holy Spirit**

**Human
Spirit**

Soul (Mind,
Emotions, Will)

Inward
Attitudes

Body
Outward
expressions
of inward
attitudes

making a moral choice to be obedient. It does what it does because it *must*. An animal does not have a morally free will, the ability to choose good or evil. Therefore God can be *functionally* pleased with his animal creation but can never be *morally* pleased, just as a man can be functionally pleased with his television set but can never be morally pleased.

God wanted His relationship with man to be a **love** relationship, received and expressed back to Him through the agency of **faith**. Therefore man had to be given a free will, because love can only be possible where it is given **freely**. Based on this love relationship, which man could have enjoyed indefinitely by his free will, God had access through Adam's spirit into his soul (teaching his mind, controlling his emotions, and directing his will) and thereby totally influenced his behavior.

As a result of this relationship, every thought, emotion, word, and deed of Adam and Eve before they rebelled was a perfect representation of the God that lived in them! They were truly fulfilling their purpose in life: walking in a dependent love relationship with their God, and through that relationship bearing a full visible expression of the invisible God.

Imagine some intelligent space creature from another planet coming to visit earth before the sin of Adam and Eve and desiring to find out what God is like. How can you see an invisible God? The best advice he could receive would be, "Man is created in the image of God. Go observe Adam and Eve, and you'll see what God is like." If he would do so, our imaginary space creature would go home with an accurate knowledge of the nature and character of God—through observing **man**, who is created in God's image.

The True Meaning
of the Fall of Man

In the Garden that God created for Adam and Eve, He placed two trees, the tree of life and the tree of the knowledge of good and evil. They were given total freedom to eat of any tree in the Garden, except for the tree of the knowledge of good and evil. God had said, "You must not eat from the tree of the knowledge of good and evil, for when you eat of it you shall surely die" (Genesis 2:17). Only God ultimately knows the difference between good and evil. As an act of love, God was showing Adam and Eve that dependence upon Him through the tree of life was the only way they could experience abundant life as He intended man to have. He was also protecting them from the choice to become their own god, which is the reason that Satan fell earlier, resulting in spiritual death.

Satan, in the form of a serpent, tempted Eve by saying, "You will not surely die. . . . For God knows that when you eat of it your eyes will be opened, and you will be like God, knowing good and evil" (Genesis 3:4,5). Adam and Eve then both took from the tree and ate, becoming their own self-appointed judges of good and evil, and setting off the entire human history of sin, suffering, and death.

It is easy for us to superficially read over this story, since it has been cartooned and lampooned so much over the years, but it is absolutely foundational to the entire Bible, and especially to our understanding of salvation. It is imperative that we clearly see both the real **meaning** of their sin and the tragic **results** of their choice.

The Meaning of Adam's Sin

While man stands apart from the rest of God's creatures, being uniquely created in His image, there is also an infinite gulf between man and God. Only God is truly independent. He needs nothing and no one, being totally self-sufficient. Man, on the other hand, is a totally **dependent** creature. He is dependent upon air, food, water, etc. for his physical life; he is dependent upon the world around him and other people for his soulish well-being; and he is dependent upon God for his spiritual life. In particular, he was created dependent upon God for his spiritual needs of **unconditional love and acceptance, and meaning and purpose in life.**

The key to the real meaning of the temptation presented to Adam and Eve lies in the serpent's phrase "in the day you eat from it . . . you will be like God." They were offered the chance (they thought) to step outside of their dependent (faith) relationship with God, and to assume an independent status—to be their own gods, to be self-sufficient.

In effect, Satan was saying, "You don't need God to be a man! If you declare your independence from God, you can be your own gods. As a god, you won't have to be subject to what God says is right and wrong. You can decide for yourself what is good and evil, and you can start right now by asserting your independence!"

The Results of Adam's Sin

Notice that God said, "In the day you eat of it, you shall surely die." They did not die *physically* that day. In fact, we are told that Adam lived a total of 930 years.

But, believing Satan's lie and calling God a liar, Adam and Eve did die *spiritually* that day! God in His holiness honored their choice to live independently from Himself. He withdrew His life from them, leaving them dead spiritually, and on their own! The promise of the serpent was a lie. Their spiritual life was not, and could not be, independent; it was a dependent life given and sustained by God. When God withdrew, they lost spiritual life and died.

NATURAL MAN
(in Adam)

Spiritually Dead—
separated from God's
Spirit and God's truth.

The man without the Spirit does not accept the things that come from the Spirit of God, for they are foolishness to him, and he cannot understand them, because they are spiritually discerned (1 Corinthians 2:14).

When Adam and Eve later had children, their offspring bore their new fallen images. You can see this in Genesis 5:1,3: "When God created man, He made him in the likeness of God. . . . When Adam had lived 130 years, he had a son in his own likeness, in his own image; and he named him Seth." The rule of reproduction is "like begets like," and two spiritually dead, sinful parents can only produce spiritually dead, sinful children. Adam could not pass on what he no longer possessed himself—spiritual life.

Romans chapter 5 amplifies this truth: "Therefore, just as sin entered the world through one man, and death through sin, and in this way death came to all men, because all sinned . . . as the result of one trespass was condemnation for all men . . . as through the disobedience of the one man the many were made sinners" (Romans 5:12,18,19). Adam actually sinned a new creature into existence, called fallen man.

As a result of Adam's choice, every person is born into this world spiritually dead and a sinner by nature. "As for you, you were dead in your transgressions and sins, in which you used to live when you followed the ways of this world and of the ruler of the kingdom of the air, the spirit who is now at work in those who are disobedient. All of us also lived among them at one time, gratifying the cravings of our sinful nature and following its desires and thoughts. Like the rest, we were by nature objects of wrath" (Ephesians 2:1-3).

Therefore, from God's point of view, **the problem of mankind is not just that they are sinners that need forgiveness; He sees a world of dead people that need life!** God's solution to both problems came through the Person of Jesus Christ.

3
CHAPTER

God in
the Flesh

The Bible clearly declares that Jesus Christ is God: "In the beginning was the Word, and the Word was with God, and the Word was God. He was with God in the beginning. Through Him all things were made; without Him nothing was made that has been made. . . . The Word became flesh and made His dwelling among us (John 1:1-3,14). While never denying or renouncing His deity, the Son of God took on a true human nature and flesh, totally identifying Himself with us in our humanity.

He was truly man, with an important difference. Since He entered the world begotten by the Holy Spirit and through the miraculous virgin birth, Jesus Christ was born **spiritually alive** and without sin. Therefore He was the **first true man** from God's point of view to live on the earth since the Fall, and thus He is known as the "second Adam": "So it is written: 'The first man Adam became a living being'; the last Adam, a life-giving spirit. . . . The first man was of the dust of the earth, the second man from heaven" (1 Corinthians 15:45,47).

Jesus Christ—God's Demonstration of True Humanity

Jesus Christ is God, has always been God, and always will be God. However, during His earthly life He did not live as God. While never denying His deity, He voluntarily assumed the limitations of humanity and lived as a man. His life was a demonstration of the way God intended every man to live—a life of **faith** and **total dependency** upon God. Listen to His own words.

> I tell you the truth, the Son can do nothing by Himself; He can do only what He sees His Father doing, because whatever the Father does the Son also does. . . . By Myself I can do nothing (John 5:19,30).

> I did not speak of My own accord, but the Father who sent Me commanded Me what to say and how to say it. I know that His command leads to eternal life. So whatever I say is just what the Father has told Me to say (John 12:49,50).

> Philip said, "Lord, show us the Father and that will be enough for us." Jesus answered: "Don't you know Me, Philip, even after I have been among you such a long time? Anyone who has seen Me has seen the Father. How can you say, 'Show us the Father'? Don't you believe that I am in the Father, and that the Father is in Me? The words I say to you are not

just My own. Rather, it is the Father, living in Me, who is doing His work. Believe Me when I say that I am in the Father and the Father is in Me; or at least believe on the evidence of the miracles themselves" (John 14:8-11).

Without ever denying His deity, Jesus Christ lived on earth in exactly the same way God intended every man to live. "But what about His miracles?" many people ask. The answer, as strange as it may sound at first, is that Jesus Christ never did a miracle simply because He was God, though God He certainly was. Every miracle performed by Christ was actually done by God the Father through Him in His role as the perfect Man!

Read carefully those verses quoted above, and notice how consistently Christ points to the Father in Him as the source of His words and works. Always His explanation is, "It isn't Me; it is the **Father** in Me who is doing **His** work." Never did Jesus step out of His role as Man and act independently or self-sufficiently. Every moment of every day of His earthly life, He walked in conscious fellowship with His Father and presented Himself to the Father for obedience. In short, Jesus Christ lived by **faith.**

For the first time since the Fall, God could be seen in man! Jesus could say, "Anyone who has seen Me has seen the Father." If anyone wanted to see what God is like, the answer was simply, "Look at Jesus of Nazareth."

However, Christ not only demonstrated what God is like, but He also demonstrated the nature of a true man. Would you like to know what a true man is, from God's point of view? Once again, the solution is, look at Jesus of Nazareth!

An Exchanged Life

To become our Savior, the Son of God first identified Himself with us in our **humanity**, "being made in human likeness" (Philippians 2:7). Then, at the cross, He totally identified Himself with us in our **sin**—"God made Him who had no sin to be sin for us" (2 Corinthians 5:21)—and even in our **death:** "Jesus called out with a loud voice, 'Father, into Your hands I commit My spirit.' When He had said this, He breathed His last" (Luke 23:46).

There was a double transaction through the cross, a total exchange. God took our sins and gave them to the sinless Christ, but that's not all. He then took His perfect righteousness and gave it to us who believe in His name. "God made Him who had no sin to be sin for us, so that in Him we might become the righteousness of God" (2 Corinthians 5:21). I often tell people, "You'll never experience a changed life until you experience the *exchanged* life." Because Christ identified Himself with us in our humanity, sin, and death, we can be identified with Him in His death, righteousness, and resurrected life.

Every Christian is profoundly grateful for the fact that Jesus Christ has decisively dealt with the sin issue, and for the mercy and grace of God that led Him to the cross. But don't leave Him there! Christianity does not center on a dead Savior, but on a **living Lord.** Salvation is more than forgiveness of sins. Christ's work of reconciliation was not an end in itself; it was a *means* to an end—the restoring of spiritual life to lost people! The whole gospel can be summed up in this statement: Jesus Christ *laid down* His life **for** you, so that He could *give* His life **to** you, so that He could *live* His life **through** you!

Salvation Is Receiving
the Life of Christ

A man I knew who was not a Christian once described his struggles to me and said, "I've asked God for help many times." My answer to him was, "That's exactly your problem. **A dead man doesn't need help. A dead man needs life!**" This is exactly what Jesus Christ offers man: "I have come that they may have life, and have it to the full" (John 10:10).

In John 5:24 Jesus said, "I tell you the truth, whoever hears My word and believes Him who sent Me has eternal life and will not be condemned; he has crossed over from death to life." He described the process of receiving this new life in terms of being "born of the Spirit": "I tell you the truth, no one can see the kingdom of God unless he is born again. . . . Flesh gives birth to flesh, but the Spirit gives birth to spirit" (John 3:3,6).

The New Testament consistently teaches that God's solution to the sin issue was the cross, but His solution to man's state of death was the **resurrection** of Christ. For example:

> Praise be to the God and Father of our Lord Jesus Christ! In His great mercy He has given us new birth into a living hope through the resurrection of Jesus Christ from the dead (1 Peter 1:3).

> When you were dead in your sins and in the uncircumcision of your sinful nature, God made you alive with Christ. He forgave us all our sins (Colossians 2:13).

> You were dead in your transgressions and sins. . . . But because of His great love for us, God, who is rich in mercy, made us alive with Christ even when we were dead in transgressions—it is by grace you have been saved. And God raised us up with Christ and seated us with Him in the heavenly realms in Christ Jesus (Ephesians 2:1,4-6).

Salvation Is Christ in You

The night before His crucifixion, Jesus told His disciples that after His departure He would send the Holy Spirit to them: "I will ask the Father, and He will give you another Counselor to be with you forever—the Spirit of truth. The world cannot accept Him, because it neither sees Him nor knows Him. But you know Him, for He lives with you and will be in you. I will not leave you as orphans; I will come to you. . . . Because I live, you also will live" (John 14:16-19).

The Lord went on to explain that through the Holy Spirit He would live in the same relationship with them in which Jesus had lived with His Father on earth: "On that day you will realize that I am in My Father, and you are in Me, and I am in you" (John 14:20).

The moment you put your faith in Jesus Christ, you step out of Adam into Christ, Christ steps out of heaven and into you, and He makes you into a new creation: "Therefore, if anyone is in Christ, he is a new creation; the old has gone, the new has come!" (2 Corinthians 5:17). Paul summed up his ministry as the proclamation of "the mystery that has been kept hidden for ages and generations, but is now disclosed to the saints . . . which is Christ in you, the hope of glory" (Colossians 1:26,27).

Being made into a "new creation" is somewhat like the caterpillar that has emerged from its cocoon as a new creature—a butterfly. As a caterpillar, it viewed life from the ground up. As a butterfly, it views life from the sky downward. In the same way, as a new creature in Christ, you must begin to see yourself **as God sees you.**

When we look at a butterfly we don't say, "There's a converted worm!" Although it was originally a worm, and it was "converted," all we now see is the beauty and grace of this new creature. The same is true of God. He only sees you as a butterfly now, **His new creation in Christ.**

Although you might not always **act** like a good "butterfly" (you sometimes land on things you shouldn't, bump into things you shouldn't, etc.), the truth of the matter is that **you are never going to be a worm again!**

This is why the usual New Testament word for a person who is in Christ is "saint," meaning "holy one." Paul wrote, for example, to "the saints in Rome," "the saints in Corinth," and "the saints in Thessalonica." Yet today I hear Christians refer to themselves as "just an old

SPIRITUAL MAN
(in Christ)

Spiritually Alive— restored to harmony with God.

Therefore, if anyone is **in Christ**, *he is a* **new creation**; *the old has gone, the new has come! (2 Corinthians 5:17).*

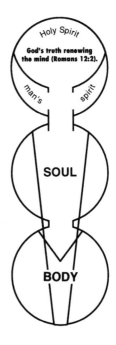

sinner saved by grace." No! That's like calling a butterfly a "converted worm." I **was** a sinner, and I **was** saved by grace, but the Word of God calls me a **saint** from the moment I was born again in Jesus Christ!

One of the greatest examples of New Testament motivation is Ephesians 5:8: "You were once darkness, but now you are light in the Lord. Live as children of light." A good paraphrase would be: "You once were a worm, but now you are a butterfly. Fly like a butterfly!"

Now, through Christ Himself living through you, you can begin to discover why God created you. You can walk with Him in a vital living relationship. You can become a vehicle for God to reveal Himself to the world. This indwelling life of Christ is revealed in us as we present ourselves to Him by faith, just as Jesus presented Himself to the Father. Paul described it this way: "I have been crucified with Christ and I no longer live, but Christ lives in me. The life I live in the body, I live by faith in the Son of God, who loved me and gave Himself for me" (Galatians 2:20).

As a child of the living God, you have been **justified** through faith in Jesus Christ: "Therefore, since we have been justified through faith, we have peace with God through our Lord Jesus Christ. . . . Since we have now been justified by His blood, how much more shall we be saved from God's wrath through Him!" (Romans 5:1,9).

The word "justified" is a court term meaning "declared totally righteous." God puts Christ's righteousness to the account of any person who puts his faith in Jesus Christ: "God made Him who had no sin [Jesus] to be sin for us, so that in Him **we might become the righteousness of God**" (2 Corinthians 5:21). We stand before God in **His** righteousness, **not our own**!

The Trap of Practical Atheism

The inheritance that is ours in Christ Jesus—our

total forgiveness, righteousness, sanctification, and gift of eternal life through the indwelling Holy Spirit— belongs to **every** child of God. It is literally true that we have received every spiritual blessing in the heavenly places in Christ (Ephesians 1:3). These things are true of every believer, regardless of his or her level of knowledge, experience, or maturity. However, it is nonetheless possible for a Christian to live as if none of these things were true, and experience very little day-to-day benefit from his union with Christ. You can be a "theoretical Christian" and live as a "practical atheist." What then is a practical atheist?

A practical atheist is someone who, regardless of his doctrinal beliefs, approaches life as if he were the only resource available.

The practical atheist reminds me of this story. A man is driving his pickup truck down a road when he meets a hitchhiker carrying a heavy load. He pulls over and offers a ride, which the hitchhiker gratefully accepts.

A little further down the road, the driver looks in the mirror and sees the hiker sitting in the bed of the truck, hunched over, still holding the load on his shoulder. The driver stops again and says, "Hey, buddy, why don't you put that pack down!"

The hitchhiker's response is, "That's okay. I don't want to bother you that much. Just take me to my destination and I'll be happy."

"How ridiculous!" you say. Yet how like many Christians that is! We happily board the Lord's "salvation wagon" that will take us to heaven, but then we continue to shoulder the effort along the way.

People say, "I don't want to bother the Lord with my little problems. I'll just talk to Him about the big ones."

I respond, "Can you imagine *God* thinking that you have a *big* problem?"

No, the error is that we see salvation as only pertaining to our eternal destiny, rather than seeing that the Christian life is **Christ's life lived out through us** each and every day.

The Vine and the Branch

This is what Jesus was pointing toward when He said, "I am the vine; you are the branches. If a man remains in Me and I in him, he will bear much fruit; apart from Me you can do nothing" (John 15:5).

The key that makes Christ's life real in our daily experience is "abiding," or **total dependence.** A branch is totally dependent upon the vine for fruit production, as well as for life itself. A branch is only a "fruit-hanger"; only the vine can *produce* fruit. A branch will *bear* fruit as it continually allows the life of the vine to flow through it (abiding), not as it "grunts and groans" in its efforts to produce fruit on its own.

Put in simple terms, abiding is "fixing our eyes on Jesus" (Hebrews 12:2) who IS (present tense) "our righteousness, holiness, and redemption" (1 Corinthians 1:30).

The attitudes of abiding are concisely described in 1 Thessalonians 5:16-18 NKJV:

> Rejoice always;
> Pray without ceasing;
> In everything give thanks,
>   for this is the will of
>   God in Christ Jesus for
>   you.

We can rejoice and give thanks in all circumstances, not because all things that happen to us are good, but because in all circumstances the love and grace of God is with us, and He has promised to cause **all things** to "work together for good to those who love God, to those who are the called according to His purpose" (Romans 8:28 NKJV).

4
CHAPTER

Locate Yourself

he most important question to ask yourself about the issues presented in this book is:

Do you know beyond the shadow of a doubt that you have received the life of Christ? Do you know for a fact that Christ Himself lives in you?

So many times on "People to People" I hear hurting individuals explain that the Christian life isn't working for them. Over and over I hear them explain that they "walked an aisle" to receive Christ, but they draw a blank when I ask if they are sure that Christ lives in them.

It always reminds me of a story that occurred to me many years ago. I worked with a man named Sid, who was an alcoholic. Sid professed to have received Christ, but his life never showed any evidence of change.

One night I received a call from Sid's wife, telling me that Sid was drunk again. I went over to visit him, and that night God showed me something I've never forgotten.

In the course of our talk I asked Sid a question I had never asked before. It went like this: "Sid, when you accepted Christ, which Jesus did you believe in?"

He looked at me with a puzzled expression. "What do you mean?"

"Did you have in your mind an honorable man named Jesus of Nazareth, who lived 2000 years ago in a place called Israel, and taught people to love one another, and eventually died on a cross? Or did you accept the Jesus Christ who is God become man, who was raised again, who is Lord, and who is alive today? The Lord Jesus Christ who offers to come and live inside you?"

Sid replied, "I received that Jesus who was a man 2000 years ago."

"Then let's get on our knees right now, Sid, and accept the *living Lord Jesus Christ*. He who is **more** than a man, who is God Himself, and who has the power to change your life from the **inside**."

We knelt together, and after we had prayed I looked into Sid's face and saw a new man! He has never taken another drink, and God that day began restoring to Sid "the years that the locust ate away." In his mid-seventies he began a new business venture, and to this day his life reveals the presence of an indwelling Lord.

What about you? I'm not saying you have to understand these things in every detail in order to be saved. God looks on the heart. However, poor evangelism that only presents half the gospel sometimes results in years of confusion in the lives of people. Satan beats them for years with the question "Did I or didn't I really believe?" Or "Did I really have enough faith?"

The answer to the uncertainty is not in digging up what you did or didn't do in the past, but in nailing down **TODAY** your acceptance of Christ Himself in you. If you are in doubt, the following prayer can answer your desire for assurance and can begin the experience of Christ in you:

> *Lord Jesus, I need You. Thank You for dying for the forgiveness of my sins. Thank You for offering me Your life. I now receive Your life and Your righteousness. Come into my heart as my Savior and Lord. As an expression of my faith, I now thank You for giving Your life to me. Now teach me to let You live Your life through me.*

5
CHAPTER

The Deity of Christ

Here is a man who was born in an obscure village, the child of a Jewish peasant woman. He grew up in another obscure village. He worked in a carpenter shop until He was 30, and then for three years He was an itinerant preacher. He never wrote a book. He never held an office. He never owned a home. He never had a family. He never went to college. He never put His foot inside a big city. He never traveled 200 miles from the place where He was born. He never did one of the things that usually accompany greatness. He had no credentials but Himself.

While still a young man, the tide of popular opinion turned against Him. His friends ran away. One of them denied Him. He was turned over to His enemies. He went through the mockery of a trial. He was nailed to a cross between two thieves. His executioners gambled for the only piece of property He had on earth while He was dying—and that was His coat. When He was dead He was taken down and laid in a borrowed grave through the pity of a friend.

Nineteen wide centuries have come and gone, and today He is the centerpiece of the human race and the leader of the column of progress. I am far within the mark when I say that all the armies that ever marched, and all the navies that ever were built, and all the parliaments that ever sat, and all the kings that ever reigned, put together have not affected the life of man upon this earth as powerfully as has the **one solitary life.**

—Author Unknown

Christianity is not a **religion**, but a **relationship** with the living Christ. You can take Buddha out of Buddhism, Muhammad out of Islam, and the founders of the various religions out of their religious systems, and little would be changed. But take Christ out of Christianity and there would be nothing left. Therefore, if we are going to become true **followers** of Christ, it is imperative that we openly and thoroughly explore the Person of Jesus Christ and His claims upon our lives.

Key Verse: John 1:1,14

In the beginning was the Word, and the Word was with God, and the Word was God. ... And the Word became flesh and dwelt among us, and we beheld His glory, the glory as of the only begotten of the Father, full of grace and truth (NKJV).

1. Who was in the beginning?

2. Who was the Word with?

3. Who was the Word?

4. What two things did the Word do?

   a)

   b)

5. Who is John referring to here?

6. Who then is the Word?

7. Who is Jesus?

Who Did Jesus Christ Claim to Be?

"My sheep listen to My voice; I know them, and they follow Me. I give them eternal life, and they shall never perish; no one can snatch them out of My hand. My Father, who has given them to Me, is greater than all; no one can snatch them out of My Father's hand. I and the Father are one." Again the Jews picked up stones to stone Him, but Jesus said to them, "I have shown you many great miracles from the Father. For which of these do you stone Me?" "We are not stoning You for any of these," replied the Jews, "but for blasphemy, because You, a mere man, claim to be God" (John 10:27-33).

1. What relationship does Jesus claim to have with the Father (verse 30)?

2. What was the reaction of the Jews to this claim (verse 31)?

3. What did they think Jesus claimed about Himself? (verse 33)?

> You are from below; I am from above. You are of this world; I am not of this world (John 8:23).

> I have come down from heaven not to do My will but to do the will of Him who sent Me (John 6:38).

> No one has seen the Father except the One who is from God; only He has seen the Father (John 6:46).

1. From where did Jesus claim to be?

2. What is the significance of Christ's claim?

> Your father Abraham rejoiced at the thought of seeing My day; he saw it and was glad. "You are not yet fifty years old," the Jews said to Him, "and You have seen Abraham!" "I tell you the truth," Jesus answered, "before Abraham was born, I am!" At this, they picked up stones to stone Him, but Jesus hid Himself,

slipping away from the temple grounds (John 8:56-59).

1. What did Jesus say about Abraham seeing His day?

2. Did this make sense to the Jews (verse 57)?

3. What did Jesus claim about Himself (verse 58)?

4. In Exodus 3:14 God told Moses to tell the Israelites "I AM WHO I AM. . . . I AM has sent me to you." How does Christ's claim concerning Himself in John 8:58 compare to what God told Moses?

5. What then was Christ claiming about Himself?

Now, Father, glorify Me in Your presence with the glory I had with You before the world began (John 17:5).

1. What did Jesus claim about Himself in this verse?

2. Could an ordinary man make these claims?

3. What is **your** reaction to these claims?

Jesus said in John 4:24 and 6:46 that "God is spirit" and that "no one has seen the Father except the One who is from God; only He has seen the Father." In the following passages, how did Jesus say that **we** can see and know God?

1. John 12:44,45.

2. John 14:7-10.

3. In these passages, what is the relationship between Jesus and the Father?

4. Who is the Father?

5. Who is Jesus?

The claims that Jesus made about Himself must be dealt with by every human being. Either He was **who He said He was** or else He was the greatest **liar** or **maniac** who ever walked upon the face of the earth. Consider the following:

If Jesus **thought** He was God and yet He was not, what would you conclude about Him?

If Jesus **knew** He was not God and yet claimed that He was, what would you conclude about Him?

What is the only other alternative?

C.S. Lewis once said, "A man who was merely a man and said the sort of things Jesus said would not be a great moral teacher. He would either be a lunatic—on a level with the man who says he is a poached egg—or else he would be the Devil of Hell. You must make your choice. Either this man was, and is, the Son of God, or else a madman or something worse. You can shut Him up for a fool, you can spit at Him and kill Him as a demon, or you can fall at His feet and call Him Lord and God. But let us not come up with any patronizing nonsense about His being a great human teacher. He has not left that open to us. He did not intend to."

Historical Evidences
for Christ's Deity

The Witness of Christ's Apostles

Those who knew Jesus personally, who walked and talked and lived with Him for three years, are unanimous in their testimony to His deity:

The apostle John: In the beginning was the Word, and the Word was with God, and the Word was God. . . . And the Word became flesh and dwelt among us, and we beheld His glory, the glory as of the only begotten of the Father, full of grace and truth (John 1:1,14 NKJV).

The apostle Paul: In Christ all the fullness of the Deity lives in bodily form (Colossians 2:9).

The apostle Peter: Through the righteousness of our God and Savior Jesus Christ (2 Peter 1:1).

The writer of Hebrews: The Son is the radiance of God's glory and the exact representation of His being, sustaining all things by His powerful word (Hebrews 1:3).

See also Philippians 2:5-11; Colossians 1:15-17; John 20:27,28; Matthew 16:16.

The Witness of
Old Testament Prophecy

Jesus Christ is the subject of more than 300 Old Testament prophecies made several hundred years before His birth. History confirms that even the smallest detail came about just as predicted.

For example, the prophet Isaiah wrote this prophecy in 700 B.C.: "Therefore the Lord Himself will give you a sign: Behold, the virgin shall conceive and bear a Son, and shall call His name Immanuel [which means 'GOD WITH US']" (Isaiah 7:14 NKJV). Matthew 1:18-23 records the fulfillment of this prophecy 700 years later by the birth of Jesus Christ in Bethlehem. The historical event of God becoming a man can be more easily understood by the following story.

A devout member of a Hindu sect was confronted with the claims of Christ. To him all life was sacred—a cow, an insect, a cobra. Yet he could not grasp the Christian concept that God actually visited this planet in the Person of Jesus Christ.

One day while walking through the field wrestling in his mind with this concept of God, he observed an anthill that was in the path of a farmer plowing the field. Gripped with the same kind of concern that you and I would feel for hundreds of people trapped in a burning building, he wanted to warn the ants of their impending danger. But how? He could shout to them, but they would not understand. He could write to them, but they could not read. How then could he communicate with them? Then the realization came: Out of sheer love he wished that *he could become an ant.* If this could have been possible, he could have warned them before it was too late.

Now at last he understood the Christian concept. God **called** to us, but we wouldn't listen. He **wrote** to us, but we refused to read. Out of sheer love He **became a man** in order to clearly communicate His love and forgiveness to us.

The Resurrection: God's Final Proof

Before the Crucifixion

Then the Jews demanded of Him, "What

miraculous sign can You show us to prove Your authority to do all this?" Jesus answered them, "Destroy this temple, and I will raise it again in three days." The Jews replied, "It has taken forty-six years to build this temple, and You are going to raise it in three days?" But the temple He had spoken of was His body. After He was raised from the dead, His disciples recalled what He had said. Then they believed the Scripture and the words that Jesus had spoken (John 2:18-22).

1. What sign does Jesus offer to prove His authority?

2. To what was Jesus referring when He said "Destroy this temple"?

3. Did His disciples understand at that time what He was talking about?

4. When did they understand what He meant?

5. What was the result of their understanding?

6. If these statements came true, what can you conclude about the other statements Jesus made?

7. What powers did Jesus claim to have, according to John 10:17,18?

_____ and _____

8. According to the previous two passages, was the crucifixion of Jesus an accident or was it foreknown and planned by God?

After the Resurrection

> On the evening of that first day of the week, when the disciples were together, with the doors locked for fear of the Jews, Jesus came and stood among them and said, "Peace be with you!" After He said this, He showed them His hands and side. The disciples were overjoyed when they saw the Lord (John 20:19,20).

1. To whom did Jesus appear, according to the above verses?

2. What was their response?

3. In verses 24 and 25, how would you describe the disciple Thomas?

4. How did his attitude change after seeing the resurrected Christ (verses 26-29)?

Historians, people trained in the laws of evidence, and others have affirmed that the resurrection of Jesus Christ is a well-established fact. Written only 25 years after the fact, 1 Corinthians 15:6 tells us that in addition to appearing to several individuals, Jesus was seen by **over 500 witnesses at one time.**

Man's Response to God's Revelation

We Must Turn to God in Faith

God has provided a way for you to be reconciled to Himself and to enter into a personal relationship with

Him: through turning from your sin of unbelief and self-sufficiency and receiving Jesus Christ as your Savior and Lord.

> It is by grace you have been saved, through faith—and this not from yourselves, it is the gift of God—not by works, so that no one can boast (Ephesians 2:8,9).

How are you saved? "By _____ through _____."

> If you **confess** with your mouth, "Jesus is Lord," and **believe** in your heart that God raised Him from the dead, you will be saved. For it is with your heart that you believe and are justified, and it is with your mouth that you confess and are saved (Romans 10:9,10).

> To all who **received** Him, to those who believed in His name, He gave the right to become children of God (John 1:12).

How do you become a child of God?

Read 1 John 5:11-13.

1. Where is eternal life to be found, according to this passage?

2. If you have the Son, what do you have?

3. Can you have one without the other?

4. Do you think you can have **eternal life** apart from **total forgiveness?**

5. What does "eternal" mean?

6. Could you ever lose something that was eternal?

7. According to the above passages, **when** does eternal life begin?

8. Therefore **when** are your sins totally forgiven?

9. In light of these scriptural truths, how can you have complete assurance regarding your salvation?

If you are not **100 percent sure** that Jesus Christ is in your life and that you have eternal life, you can be sure once and for all right now.

Prayer is man's way of talking with God (confessing with your mouth that Jesus is Lord). God is not so concerned with your **words** as He is with the **attitude of your heart (believing in your heart that God raised Him from the dead).** Would you like to pray right now and ask Christ to come into your heart once and for all and make you what He wants you to be?

> Lord Jesus, in faith I turn to You as 100 percent sufficient for my salvation, realizing that there is nothing I can do to add to what You did for me at the cross. I thank You for the total forgiveness of all my sins, for giving me eternal life, and for giving me Your righteousness. I thank You that You now live in my

heart and that I never have to doubt it again, and that the life I now live I live by faith in the Son of God, who loved me and delivered Himself up for me.

Were you sincere when you prayed this prayer? If so, the living **Christ has come to dwell within you FOREVER,** you have been **reconciled to God,** all of your sins have been **forgiven forever,** and you have begun the great adventure for which you were created as a **child of God.** Begin today to trust God by thanking Him every day for His total forgiveness for your sins and for your everlasting relationship with the living God.

We Cannot Depend on Feelings

Faith must have a **foundation.** The foundation of the Christian's faith is **Christ and His Word.** Our faith is based upon **fact** (God and His Word), not upon our **feelings** concerning God and His Word.

Fact: Christ said He will come into your heart and forgive your sins if you ask Him to.

Faith: Your personal trust in what He said He would do.

Feeling: If you asked Christ into your life, He **has come** to live in you **regardless** of your feelings.

6
CHAPTER

The Authority of Scripture

N o book in history can equal the impact of the Bible upon individuals and nations. The Bible has been printed, read, translated, revered, and attacked more than any other writing.

The Bible has stood through the centuries against vicious criticism and minute examination without being shaken. On the contrary, every spade turned by archae-ologists provides further confirmation of the historical accuracy and integrity of the Bible.

However, the primary reason for placing ourselves under scriptural authority is not the Bible's uniqueness or accuracy, or even its power to change lives. Nor is it because the church has universally accepted the Bible's divine inspiration and authority for more than 1800 years. Rather, the supreme reason for accepting the inspiration of the Bible and its authority over our lives is because of **our faith in Jesus Christ and His testimony concerning the Word of God.**

Earlier in this book we established the fact that Jesus Christ is God: "In Christ all the fullness of the Deity lives in bodily form" (Colossians 2:9). If Jesus Christ is not

God, then it makes little difference what the Bible says, because man is still in his sins. However, if He is God, then our attitude toward the Bible must be determined by what **He** said about it, and not by what the world says.

The answer to the question "What do you think about the Bible?" rests entirely on the answer to the question that Jesus asked His disciples: "Who do you say I am?" (Matthew 16:15).

Key Verse: 1 John 1:1,3

That which was from the beginning, which we have heard, which we have seen with our eyes, which we have looked at and our hands have touched—this we proclaim concerning the Word of life. . . . We proclaim to you what we have seen and heard, so that you also may have fellowship with us.

1. What four things qualified the apostles to testify about the Word of life?

   a)

   b)

   c)

   d)

2. Would John's statement lead you to believe that he is recording historical facts?

3. To whom does the "Word of life" refer?

4. What relationship do you see between this verse and John 1:1?

The Authority of the Old Testament

Christ's Claims About the Old Testament

> You diligently study the Scriptures because you think that by them you possess eternal life. These are the Scriptures that testify about Me, yet you refuse to come to Me to have life (John 5:39,40).

1. Why did the Jews diligently study the Scriptures?

2. What did Jesus say these Scriptures testify about?

3. What Scriptures is He talking about?

4. Does Jesus indicate in this passage that He believes the Old Testament is true?

> If you believed Moses, you would believe Me, for he wrote about Me. But since you do not believe what he wrote, how are you going to believe what I say? (John 5:46,47).

1. Of whom did Jesus say that Moses wrote in the above verses?

2. How did Jesus equate believing in Moses' writings and believing His own words?

3. According to the above passages, what was Jesus' attitude toward the Old Testament?

4. What should our attitude be?

5. If someone rejects the validity of the Old Testament, what is he or she in effect saying about Jesus?

Christ's Witness to Old Testament Events

Christ validated the old Testament account of Noah and the flood.

> As it was in the days of Noah, so it will be at the coming of the Son of Man. For in the days before the flood, people were eating and drinking, marrying and giving in marriage, up to the day Noah entered the ark: and they knew nothing about what would happen until the flood came and took them all away. That is how it will be at the coming of the Son of Man (Matthew 24:37-39).

1. How many people were destroyed by the flood?

2. Did Jesus state this as an actual account or as a mythical or allegorical story?

3. If this account in the Old Testament had been wrong, do you think Jesus (who is God) would have corrected it?

4. To what future event does He compare the days of Noah?

5. Would it make sense to compare such an important event as the second coming of Christ to a mythical story?

6. If one story were false, what would you have to conclude about the other?

Christ validated the Old Testament account of Jonah and the big fish.

> Some of the Pharisees and teachers of the law said to Him, "Teacher, we want to see a miraculous sign from you." He answered, "A wicked and adulterous generation asks for a miraculous sign! But none will be given it except the sign of the prophet Jonah. For as Jonah was three days and three nights in the belly of a huge fish, so the Son of Man will be three days and three nights in the heart of the earth. The men of Nineveh will stand up at the judgment with this generation and condemn it; for they repented at the preaching of Jonah, and now one greater than Jonah is here" (Matthew 12:38-41).

1. Jesus claimed to be greater than whom?

2. Would it have any meaning to claim to be greater than someone who did not exist?

3. Does Jesus indicate by His statement that He believed Jonah was a historical person and this was a historical event?

4. What then can **you** conclude about the account of Jonah in the huge fish?

If Jesus Christ is **God** and He said there was a flood, **then there was a flood!** If He said Jonah was swallowed by a huge fish, **then he was!** If Jesus is **not** God, then we are still lost in our sins, and whether or not there was a flood or a huge fish is completely irrelevant to our lives.

There are at least **66 references** to the Old Testament in Christ's dialogues with the disciples and **more than 90 references** to it in His speaking with other people. There was never any question in the mind of Christ or the writers of the New Testament about the veracity of the Scriptures, nor did their enemies even challenge it. The validity and significance of these Old Testament events rests squarely upon the validity of the testimony of Jesus and the apostles.

The Authority of the New Testament

You also must testify, for you have been with Me from the beginning (John 15:27).

1. What did Jesus say the disciples must do?

2. What gave the disciples the authority to bear witness to Christ and write the New Testament, according to this passage?

It is important to realize that the writers of the New Testament were men who had been with the Lord Jesus "beginning from John's baptism to the time when Jesus was taken up from us . . . [and] must become a witness with us of His resurrection" (Acts 1:22). This includes Paul, who witnessed the resurrected Christ in a unique way (1 Corinthians 15:5-8).

> The Counselor, the Holy Spirit, whom the Father will send in My name, will teach you all things and will remind you of everything I have said to you (John 14:26).

1. What did Christ say the Holy Spirit would do for the apostles?

2. How much would He teach them?

3. How much of what Christ said to them while abiding with them would the Holy Spirit bring back to their memory?

> Then the Jews demanded of Him, "What miraculous sign can You show us to prove Your authority to do all this?" Jesus answered them, "Destroy this temple, and I will raise it again in three days." The Jews replied, "It has taken forty-six years to build this temple, and You are going to raise it in three days?" But the temple He had spoken of was His body. After He was raised from the dead, His disciples recalled what He had said. Then they believed

the Scripture and the words that Jesus had spoken (John 2:18-22).

1. This passage provides an example of Christ's promise of remembrance. What did the disciples remember (verse 22)?

2. What did they believe?

3. When did they remember and believe these things?

> I have much more to say to you, more than you can now bear. But when He, the Spirit of truth, comes, He will guide you into all truth. He will not speak on His own; He will speak only what He hears, and He will tell you what is yet to come. He will bring glory to Me by taking from what is Mine and making it known to you (John 16:12-14).

1. What did Christ say that the Holy Spirit would do for the apostles (verse 13)?

2. Whom does the Holy Spirit bring glory to?

3. What did Christ say the Holy Spirit would make known to the apostles?

4. In light of the above passages, how did God ensure that John and the other writers would accurately record His revelations?

5. Why then can we accept the authority of the New Testament with complete confidence?

The apostle Peter summed it up when he wrote:

> Above all, you must understand that no prophecy of Scripture came about by the prophet's own interpretation. For prophecy never had its origin in the will of man, but men spoke from God as they were carried along by the Holy Spirit (2 Peter 1:20,21).

The last 27 books of the Bible, called the New Testament, contain the records of the Person of Jesus Christ and of the events leading up to and following His death and resurrection. The apostles who penned these accounts did not record their own ideas and impressions, but what they actually saw and heard as they walked and talked with Jesus, and what He supernaturally inspired.

Understanding the Word of God

1. According to John 14:6, what is truth?

2. What did Jesus say is truth in John 17:17?

3. Therefore where will the Holy Spirit always lead the believer for truth?

> All Scripture is God-breathed and is useful for teaching, rebuking, correcting and training in righteousness, so that the man of

God may be thoroughly equipped for every good work (2 Timothy 3:16,17).

1. How much Scripture is given by inspiration from God (God-breathed)?

2. How is it useful to us?

3. What will be the personal results in our lives?

4. Since the Holy Spirit is our teacher (John 14:26), can every child of God read and understand the Bible?

The Bible answers life's most important questions: Who is God and what is He like? What does He expect from us? Who are we and why are we here?

In addition to answering these central questions, the Bible teaches us how to live a full and meaningful life. It instructs us on how to enjoy our daily life and how to live above the circumstances rather than be buried underneath them. The Word of God gives us practical counsel on how to get along with our families, our friends, and even our enemies.

The Bible is an autobiography of God, a study in human behavior, a historical account, a counselor's manual, a textbook on life, a telescope into the future, a storehouse of riches, and a love letter. It is a library of answers given to us out of the heart of a loving God; it contains all the riches and treasures He has given to us as His children. The Word of God can fulfill every human need, and that is why it is important for us to learn how to use this very unique Book.

An interesting period in the life of Billy Graham, world-renowned evangelist, illustrates the necessity for every child of God to individually come to grips with the authority of the Bible. Through the influence of a close friend who harbored serious doubts about the integrity of the Scriptures, and through extensive reading of other men's opinions on theological questions, Mr. Graham found himself growing more and more confused about his own view of the Bible. Was the Bible still to be accepted as an infallible standard even in the face of problems too hard to resolve? Could he continue to trust a gospel message that came from a book that was questioned by many intelligent, educated men? These questions plagued him for a long time.

Finally, in the summer of 1949, while attending a conference in Forest Home, California, Mr. Graham had a final confrontation with God. As John Pollock recorded in _Billy Graham: The Authorized Biography_:

> [Mr. Graham] saw that intellect alone could not resolve the question of authority. He must go beyond intellect. He thought of the faith used constantly in daily life; he did not know how a train or a plane or a car worked, but he rode them. He did not know why a brown cow could eat green grass and yield white milk, but he drank milk. Was it only in the things of the Spirit that such faith was wrong?
>
> "So I went back and I got my Bible, and I went out in the moonlight. And I got to a stump and put the Bible on the stump, and I

knelt down, and I said, 'Oh, God; I cannot prove certain things. I cannot answer some of the questions...people are raising, but I accept this Book by faith as the Word of God.'"

This incident was immediately followed by the largest evangelistic campaign of Billy Graham's entire ministry, one that launched him into a worldwide ministry.

Have **you** ever personally accepted by faith the entire Bible as the Word of God? The following is a suggested prayer:

Father, thank You for leaving Your holy Word with us. Thank You for giving me Your Spirit so I can understand the very mind of God as revealed in Your Word. Beginning today I accept by faith the authority of the Word of God over my life, and I trust it without reserve as Your personal Word to me.

As the apostle Paul said, "So then, just as you received Christ Jesus as Lord, continue to live in Him, rooted and built up in Him, strengthened in the faith as you were taught, and overflowing with thankfulness" (Colossians 2:6,7).

7
CHAPTER

Christ's Finished Work

P opular in the world's philosophy today is the idea that man is basically good and, if given enough time, he will improve. One adherent to this philosophy was Dr. Cyril E.M. Joad, head of the philosophy department of the University of London. Dr. Joad believed that Jesus was only a man, and that God was simply a part of the universe. He believed that there is no such thing as sin, and that, given a little time, man would have heaven on earth.

In his later life, however, after having been antagonistic toward Christianity, Dr. Joad came to believe that sin was a reality. Two world wars and the ever-present threat of another war had demonstrated conclusively to him that man was sinful. Before his death Dr. Joad became a zealous follower of the Savior, believing that the only explanation for sin was found in the Word of God, and the only solution was found in the cross of Jesus Christ.

Man throughout the ages has continually sought a life of freedom and happiness through many ways: financial success, social status, education, sexual encounters,

friends, marriage and children, approval of others, occu-
pation, and profession. However, many people have
achieved all of these things and still have not found a
meaningful and happy life. Man has even turned to
religion and social reform in an attempt to fill the void in
his life. However, even such a man as the great Hindu
leader Mahatma Gandhi, with his undying and sacrificial
devotion to his religion, stated in his autobiography: "It
is a constant torture to me that I am still so far from Him
whom I know to be my very life and being. I know it is my
own wretchedness and wickedness that keeps me from
Him."

There is a basic need in the heart of every person to
know God, to experience His forgiveness, and to be freed
from the bondage of guilt. The French philosopher Pascal
summed it up when he said, "There is a God-shaped
vacuum in the heart of every man which cannot be filled
by any created thing, but only by God the Creator, made
known through Jesus Christ."

Key Verse: 2 Corinthians 5:18,19

All this is from God, who reconciled us
to Himself through Christ and gave us the
ministry of reconciliation: that God was reconciling the world to Himself in Christ, not
counting men's sins against them. And He has
committed to us the message of reconciliation.

1. What has God done for us through Christ?

2. What was necessary for God to do in order to
   accomplish reconciliation?

3. Do you believe that God is not counting your sins against you?

4. Once we have been reconciled to God, what kind of work does He assign to us?

God Wants Everyone to Be Reconciled to Himself

Why did God desire man to be reconciled to Him, according to these verses?

> For God so loved the world that He gave His one and only Son, that whoever believes in Him shall not perish but have eternal life (John 3:16).

> This is how God showed His love among us: He sent His one and only Son into the world that we might live through Him. This is love: not that we loved God, but that He loved us and sent His Son as an atoning sacrifice for our sins (1 John 4:9,10).

Webster defines "reconcile" as a verb meaning "to restore harmony, friendship or communion." The Greek word translated "reconcile" in 2 Corinthians 5:18,19 qualifies this definition in that only **one** person in a relationship has turned away and needs to be restored. It is **man** who has turned away and become enemies with God. Throughout all of mankind's rebellious history, God has continued to love man and desire that he be reconciled to Himself, that they "be made friends" again. It was God's heart of love and desire for reconciliation that led Him to take the costly measures necessary to redeem mankind.

Why Man Needs to Be Reconciled to God

1. What does 1 John 1:8,10 say about man?

2. What is the sin of the world, according to John 16:9?

I tell you the truth, whoever hears My word and believes Him who sent Me has eternal life and will not be condemned; he has crossed over from death to life (John 5:24).

1. What do you have if you believe in the Father who sent Jesus?

2. Will you ever be judged?

3. What is the state of the unbeliever, according to this verse?

Reconciliation Requires Total Forgiveness

It was God's desire that all people be reconciled to Himself (Colossians 1:19-22). Because sin is what separates man from God, reconciliation could only be accomplished by providing a way whereby people's sins could be forgiven. This was accomplished from beginning to end by the sacrificial death of Jesus Christ on the cross. God "made Him who had no sin to be sin for us, so that in Him we might become the righteousness of God" (2 Corinthians 5:21). **Our** sin was judged in **His** body, and we were set free. The forgiveness obtained by Christ's death on the cross was not an **end** in itself; rather, it was the **means of accomplishing the end**—that of reconciliation. Therefore, after total forgiveness had been accomplished through the cross, our Lord could cry out with complete authority, "It is finished!" (John 19:30). Reconciliation had been accomplished once and for all.

1. How did John the Baptist describe Jesus in John 1:29?

2. What did God do about your sins, according to 1 John 2:12?

   Why did He forgive them?

3. Why did Christ come to earth, according to 1 John 3:5?

   Why was He able to die for our sins?

4. In light of these passages, how does the believer appear before God?

5. Once total forgiveness has been gained, is there anything else to be done for sin?

6. Could you have total forgiveness apart from Christ?

   Could you have Christ without having total forgiveness?

The Word of God says, "By one sacrifice He has made perfect forever those who are being made holy" (Hebrews 10:14), and "Their sins and lawless acts I will remember no more. And where these have been forgiven, **there is no longer any sacrifice for sin**" (Hebrews 10:17,18).

The diagram on the next page illustrates how Christ provided **total** forgiveness for **all** of man's sins.

Reconciliation Requires a New Birth

Jesus declared, "I tell you the truth, no one can see the kingdom of God unless he is born again." "How can a man be born when he is old?" Nicodemus asked. "Surely he cannot enter a second time into his mother's womb to be born!" Jesus answered, "I tell you the truth, no one can enter the kingdom of God unless he is born of water and the Spirit. Flesh gives birth to flesh, but the Spirit gives birth to spirit (John 3:3-6).

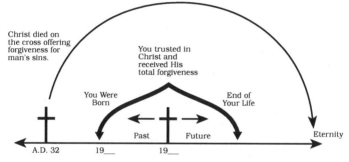

The heavy line represents the extent of Christ's forgiveness for your sins—from the moment of your birth to your death.

1. What did Jesus say must happen before a person can see the kingdom of God?

2. What kind of birth is it (verse 6)?

   To all who received Him, to those who believed in His name, He gave the right to become children of God—children born not of natural descent, nor of human decision or a husband's will, but born of God (John 1:12,13).

1. How do you become a child of God (be born again)?

2. To what does John equate receiving Christ?

3. Does your natural birth have anything to do with being born of God?

> All that the Father gives Me will come to Me, and whoever comes to Me I will never drive away. For I have come down from heaven not to do My will but to do the will of Him who sent Me. And this is the will of Him who sent Me, that I shall lose none of all that He has given Me, but raise them up at the last day. For My Father's will is that everyone who looks to the Son and believes in Him shall have eternal life, and I will raise him up at the last day (John 6:37-40).

1. Will Jesus ever reject a person who believes in Him?

2. According to verses 39 and 40, will any of those who have experienced the new birth ever be lost again?

3. According to John 11:25,26, is it possible for a person who has been born again to die spiritually?

4. How does God's promise in 1 John 5:14,15 give assurance to the one who asks eternal life of God?

Results of the New Birth

In addition to being totally forgiven, the Christian has inherited a wonderful position before God that is as permanent and secure as his salvation. The Word of God clearly testifies to the Christian's inheritance.

Saved by grace: "It is by grace you have been saved, through faith—and this not from yourselves, it is the gift of God—not by works, so that no one can boast" (Ephesians 2:8,9).

Totally forgiven: "When you were dead in your sins and in the uncircumcision of your sinful nature, God made you alive with Christ. He forgave us all our sins, having canceled the written code, with its regulations, that was against us and that stood opposed to us; He took it away, nailing it to the cross" (Colossians 2:13,14).

Reconciled to God: "If, when we were God's enemies, we were reconciled to Him through the death of His Son, how much more, having been reconciled, shall we be saved through His life!" (Romans 5:10).

Justified: "All have sinned and fall short of the glory of God, and are justified freely by His grace through the redemption that came by Christ Jesus" (Romans 3:23,24).

Made into a new creature: "Therefore, if anyone is in Christ, he is a new creation; the old has gone, the new has come!" (2 Corinthians 5:17).

Made at peace with God: "Therefore, since we have been justified through faith, we have peace with God through our Lord Jesus Christ" (Romans 5:1).

Made righteous: "God made Him who had no sin to be sin for us, so that in Him we might become the righteousness of God" (2 Corinthians 5:21).

Made perfect forever: "By one sacrifice He has made perfect forever those who are being made holy" (Hebrews 10:14).

Freed from condemnation: "Therefore there is now no condemnation for those who are in Christ Jesus" (Romans 8:1).

Made holy and blameless: "Now He has reconciled you by Christ's physical body through death to present you holy in His sight, without blemish and free from accusation" (Colossians 1:22).

Freed from the law: "Through Christ Jesus the law of the Spirit set me free from the law of sin and death" (Romans 8:2).

Hidden with Christ in God: "You died, and your life is now hidden with Christ in God" (Colossians 3:3).

Clothed with Christ: "All of you who were baptized into Christ have clothed yourselves with Christ" (Galatians 3:27).

Note: To be "clothed with Christ" means that whenever God looks at the believer He sees the righteousness of Jesus Christ.

Loved perfectly: "I am convinced that neither death nor life, neither angels nor demons, neither the present nor the future, nor any powers, neither height nor depth, nor anything else in all creation, will be able to separate us from the love of God that is in Christ Jesus our Lord" (Romans 8:38,39).

Living by Faith in Christ's Finished Work on the Cross

1. What did Jesus say was the sin of the world (John 16:9)?

2. How is the child of God to live, according to John 6:28,29?

Romans 12:2 tells us, "Do not conform any longer to the pattern of this world, but be transformed by the renewing of your mind."

Why don't you bow your head right now and, as an act of your will, claim by faith the finished work of Christ in your life. The following is a suggested prayer.

> *Lord Jesus, I thank You for all that You accomplished on the cross for me—my reconciliation with God, the total forgiveness of all my sins, and the new position of righteousness that I have before You. Thank You for showing me that Your finished work on the cross was so complete that there is nothing I can do to add to it and nothing I can do to take away from it. Let me walk from this day onward in the knowledge of Your love and grace for me.*

Learning to walk in Christ's finished work on the cross can best be accomplished by beginning to claim by faith the truths contained in the acrostic **ACTS.**

God's Pattern for Experiencing Freedom in the Spirit

A̲bide in the love and grace of Jesus Christ: "Their sins and lawless acts I will remember no more. And where these have been forgiven, there is no longer any sacrifice for sin" (Hebrews 10:17,18).

"God made Him who had no sin to be sin for us, so that in Him we might become the righteousness of God" (2 Corinthians 5:21).

"I am convinced that neither death nor life, neither angels nor demons, neither the present nor the future, nor any powers, neither height nor depth, nor anything else in all creation, will be able to separate us from the love of God that is in Christ Jesus our Lord" (Romans 8:38,39).

C̲laim by faith your total dependency upon Christ: "I am the vine; you are the branches. If a man remains in Me and I in him, he will bear much fruit; apart from Me you can do nothing" (John 15:5).

"It is God who works in you to will and to act according to His good purpose" (Philippians 2:13).

"Not that we are competent in ourselves to claim anything for ourselves, but our competence comes from God" (2 Corinthians 3:5).

Thank God in all things: "What a wretched man I am! Who will rescue me from this body of death? Thanks be to God—through Jesus Christ our Lord!" (Romans 7:24,25a).

"Give thanks in all circumstances, for this is God's will for you in Christ Jesus" (1 Thessalonians 5:18).

"We know that in all things God works for the good of those who love Him, who have been called according to His purpose" (Romans 8:28).

Stand firm in your position in Christ: "By one sacrifice He has made perfect forever those who are being made holy" (Hebrews 10:14).

"Therefore there is now no condemnation for those who are in Christ Jesus" (Romans 8:1).

"Therefore if anyone is in Christ, he is a new creation; the old has gone, the new has come!" (2 Corinthians 5:17).

"It is for freedom that Christ has set us free. Stand firm, then, and do not let yourselves be burdened again by a yoke of slavery" (Galatians 5:1).

8

CHAPTER

The Indwelling of
the Holy Spirit

J esus said, "I came that they might have life, and might have it abundantly" (John 10:10). The good news of the gospel is not just that Christ came to **die for you**, but that He also came to **live in you.** Galatians 2:20 puts it this way: "I have been crucified with Christ and I no longer live, but Christ lives in me. The life I live in the body, I live by faith in the Son of God, who loved me and gave Himself for me." Misunderstanding of this spiritual truth can enslave you to the impossible task of trying to live the Christian life yourself rather than **allowing Christ to live His life in and through you.** The inevitable failure of such an attempt will bring you to the practical conclusion that Christianity does not work.

However, the moment we come to the Lord Jesus Christ in saving faith, God gives us everything we would ever need to live rich, full lives. He does this by sending His Holy Spirit to live in us. It is therefore imperative that the Christian learn who the Holy Spirit is and what He does in the life of a believer.

Key Verse: John 16:7

I tell you the truth: It is for your good that I am going away. Unless I go away, the Counselor will not come to you; but if I go, I will send Him to you.

1. What is Jesus' attitude toward leaving His disciples?

2. Why is it good for Him to go away?

3. Did Jesus consider it better for us to have Him physically living here **with** us or the Holy Spirit living **within** us?

4. Why do you think this is better?

Who Is the Holy Spirit?

It is essential to understand who the Holy Spirit is before we can understand the work or ministry of the Holy Spirit in the life of a believer. The Word of God provides the answers to both of these issues.

Acts 5:1-4 presents a revealing incident about the identity of the Holy Spirit. A man named Ananias had sold some personal property and brought a portion of the proceeds to the church, while claiming that it was the **total** price received. The apostle Peter reproved Ananias for this deception and said, "Ananias, why has Satan filled your heart to lie to the Holy Spirit, and to keep back some of the price of the land? You have not lied to men, but to GOD."

1. Whom did Peter tell Ananias he had lied to?

   _____ and _____

2. What do you conclude about the identity of the Holy Spirit?

You cannot lie to an inanimate object or an impersonal force or a divine "influence." You can only lie to a **person**. The Holy Spirit is a **Person** possessing all the characteristics of a human personality as well as all the divine attributes ascribed to God the Father and God the Son. The Holy Spirit has intellect, emotions, and will.

> I will ask the Father, and he will give you another Counselor to be with you forever—the Spirit of truth. The world cannot accept Him, because it neither sees Him nor knows Him. But you know Him, for He lives with you and will be in you (John 14:16-17).

1. How did Christ refer to the Holy Spirit?

   _____ and _____

2. What personal pronouns did Christ use in referring to the Holy Spirit?

   _____ and _____

3. Where did He say the Holy Spirit would live (abide)?

> Jesus replied, "If anyone loves Me, he will obey My teaching. My Father will love him,

and We will come to him and make Our home with him (John 14:23).

Who did Jesus say would live in us?

_____ and _____

If anyone acknowledges that Jesus is the Son of God, God lives in him and he in God (1 John 4:15).

1. Who lives in the believer, according to 1 John 4:15?

2. In summary, who lives (abides) in the believer?

   a)

   b)

   c)

   d)

3. What do you conclude is the relationship between God and the Father, Son, and the Holy Spirit?

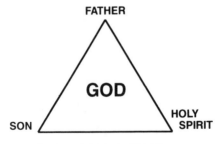

The Holy Spirit is the Third Person of the Trinity, coequal with God the Father and God the Son.

An example of a trinity in other areas of life is seen in something as basic as water, H_2O. H_2O can be a liquid, a solid, or a vapor, depending upon whether it is water, ice, or steam. Which one is H_2O?

The same is true of an egg. An egg consists of a yolk, a white, and a shell. Which one is the egg?

These illustrations are of course limited, but they help in showing how one essence can exist in three separate forms.

Our finite minds cannot understand all that is involved in the mysteries of God. The Bible clearly declares that God has revealed Himself in **three** distinct Persons, and yet it also declares that there is only **one** God. We must therefore conclude that **the sum total of the three equals the one** ($1 \times 1 \times 1 = 1$, not $1 + 1 + 1 = 3$).

In light of the evidence, we have only two options: Either the Bible is contradicting itself or else the Father and the Son and the Holy Spirit are each uniquely and totally God.

Why Did the Holy Spirit Come?

Before Salvation

One vital ministry of the Holy Spirit is to point people to Christ.

> I tell you the truth: It is for your good that I am going away. Unless I go away, the Counselor will not come to you; but if I go, I will send Him to you. When He comes, He will convict the world of guilt in regard to sin and

righteousness and judgment: in regard to sin, because men do not believe in Me; in regard to righteousness, because I am going to the Father, where you can see Me no longer (John 16:7-10).

1. What did the Holy Spirit come to do, according to John 16:7-10?

   a)

   b)

   c)

2. What did Christ say was the world's sin in verse 9?

3. What do you think verse 10 means?

4. Where is righteousness found, according to 1 John 2:1?

5. What has happened to Satan, the ruler of this world (John 16:11)?

At Salvation

Another vital ministry of the Holy Spirit is to give the believer new life.

In reply Jesus declared, "I tell you the truth, no one can see the kingdom of God unless he is born again." "How can a man be born when he is old?" Nicodemus asked. "Surely he cannot enter a second time into his mother's womb to be born!" Jesus answered, "I tell you the truth, no one can enter the kingdom of God unless he is born of water and the Spirit. Flesh gives birth to flesh, but the Spirit gives birth to spirit (John 3:3-6).

1. What is necessary in order for a person to see the kingdom of God?

2. What kind of new birth is Jesus talking about?

3. Would it be possible to belong to Christ without having the Holy Spirit within you?

When the Spirit of God comes to live in the believer it means that the Person of the Holy Spirit comes to dwell in the believer. This means that we have the mind of God (1 Corinthians 2:16), the emotions of God (Galatians 5:16,17), and the will of God (Philippians 2:13) living in us.

The Holy Spirit also enables the believer to understand the mind of God.

The Spirit searches all things, even the deep things of God. For who among men knows the thoughts of a man except the man's spirit within him? In the same way no one knows the thoughts of God except the Spirit of God. We have not received the spirit of the world but the Spirit who is from God, **that we may understand what God has freely given us** (1 Corinthians 2:10b-12).

1. What have we received?

2. What is the benefit of having God's Spirit?

After Salvation

It is the Holy Spirit who leads the believer into all truth.

1. What did the Holy Spirit come to do in John 16:13?

2. What is truth, according to John 14:6?

3. What does Jesus say is truth in John 17:17?

4. Therefore where will the Holy Spirit be leading you?

5. What is the function of the Holy Spirit, according to John 16:14?

Note: The Holy Spirit did not come to glorify Himself, but to **glorify Jesus Christ.** Anyone who is controlled by the Holy Spirit will be glorifying Christ by living by faith in His love and grace for us.

What Does It Mean to Be Filled with the Spirit?

To Be Controlled by the Love and Grace of God

God gives us His Spirit so we might understand the mind of God and the love and grace He has freely given us. The apostle Paul prayed that God would "strengthen you with power through His Spirit in your inner being, so that Christ may dwell in your hearts through faith. And I pray that you, being rooted and established in love, may have power, together with all the saints, to grasp how wide and long and high and deep is the love of Christ, and to know this love that surpasses knowledge—**that you may be filled to the measure of all the fullness of God"** (Ephesians 3:16-19).

To be filled with the Spirit means to be controlled by the love and grace of God that is found in Christ Jesus. It is only as we yield in complete abandonment to this truth that we can ever experience the fullness of God in our lives.

A mind that is set firmly upon the love and grace of God will ultimately be controlled by the love and grace of God: "The mind of sinful man is death, but the mind controlled by the Spirit is life and peace" (Romans 8:6). If you are continually filling your mind with the thoughts of the Spirit, you will ultimately be controlled by the desires of the Spirit; and He desires that you be filled to the measure with the knowledge of God's love for you and that His love will be expressed through you to the world around you. "Christ's love compels us, because we are convinced that one died for all, and therefore all died" (2 Corinthians 5:14).

To Live by Faith Daily

> I have told you these things, so that in Me you may have peace. In this world you will have trouble. But take heart! I have overcome the world (John 16:33).

1. What did Jesus say the Christian would have in this world, according to John 16:33?

2. What does Jesus promise you in the midst of trouble?

> Peace I leave with you; my peace I give you. I do not give to you as the world gives. Do not let your hearts be troubled and do not be afraid (John 14:27).

1. In John 14:27, what did Jesus say the Christian's attitude should be toward fear and anxiety?

2. What did He leave us in place of fear and anxiety?

God's Daily Provision

> God has not given us a spirit of fear, but of power and of love and of a sound mind (2 Timothy 1:7 NKJV).

> Come to Me, all you who are weary and burdened, and I will give you rest. Take My yoke upon you and learn from Me, for I am gentle and humble in heart, and you will find rest for your souls. For My yoke is easy and My burden is light (Matthew 11:28-30).

> Do not be anxious about anything, but in everything, by prayer and petition, with

thanksgiving, present your requests to God.
And the peace of God, which transcends all
understanding, will guard your hearts and
your minds in Christ Jesus (Philippians 4:6,7).

Cast all your anxiety on Him because He
cares for you (1 Peter 5:7).

My God will meet all your needs according
to His glorious riches in Christ Jesus (Philippians 4:19).

We know that in all things God works for
the good of those who love Him, who have
been called according to His purpose (Romans
8:28).

Walking Daily by Faith
in God's Love

**Faith is an action taken on the part of man toward a
promise made by God.**

Everything that does not come from **faith**
is sin (Romans 14:23b).

Without **faith** it is impossible to please
God, because anyone who comes to Him must
believe that He exists and that He rewards
those who earnestly seek Him (Hebrews 11:6).

The just shall live by **faith** (Hebrews 10:38a
NKJV).

To be filled with the Spirit is to trust God's love and His involvement in your life throughout each day. It is living with the realization that you cannot live the Christian life; **only Christ can live it through you.**

It is God's will that you understand the fullness of His love for you.

> I pray that you, being rooted and established in love, may have power, together with all the saints, to grasp how wide and long and high and deep is the love of Christ, and to know this love that surpasses knowledge—that you may be filled to the measure of all the fullness of God (Ephesians 3:17b-19).

God has promised in His Word to answer our prayers when we pray according to His will.

> This is the confidence that we have in Him, that if we ask anything according to His will, He hears us. And if we know that He hears us, whatever we ask, we know that we have the petitions that we have asked of Him (1 John 5:14,15 NKJV).

Are you willing to claim by faith God's unconditional love and total provision for you? Are you willing to be controlled by His love by trusting Him with every detail of your life? If so, you can claim the fullness of His Spirit right now in your life. The following is a suggested prayer.

> *Father, I confess that I have been in control of my life and have stopped trusting You to complete*

the work that You began in me. I thank You for Your total forgiveness provided for me by Christ Jesus. I thank You that He has become my righteousness and that, as a result, I can stand before You perfect in Your sight. I thank You that because of Your love I can trust You with every detail of my life. I now yield myself to Your control and allow You to live Your life in and through me as You continue to fill me with the knowledge of Your love and grace.

Were you sincere when you prayed this prayer? If so, you have begun the great adventure of **living by faith** in the One who loved you and gave Himself for you.

Abiding in Christ

The apostle Paul prayed in Philippians 1:9-11, "That your love may abound more and more in knowledge and depth of insight, so that you may be able to discern what is best and may be pure and blameless until the day of Christ, filled with the fruit of righteousness that comes through Jesus Christ." In Colossians 1:9-14 he prayed that God would "fill you with the knowledge of His will through all spiritual wisdom and understanding. And we pray this in order that you may live a life worthy of the Lord and may please Him in every way: bearing fruit in every good work, growing in the knowledge of God, being strengthened with all power according to His glorious might so that you may have great endurance and patience, and joyfully giving thanks to the Father, who has qualified you to share in the inheritance of the saints in the kingdom of light. For He has rescued us from the dominion of darkness and brought us into the kingdom of the Son He loves, in whom we have redemption, the forgiveness of sins."

Although the Christian's position in Christ has been established forever, sin is still a reality in his daily experience. It is therefore imperative for the Christian to understand the source of sin, the conflict of sin, and how to deal with sin when it occurs in his daily life. It is only by understanding these truths based upon the clear teaching of the Word of God that he will ever experience the freedom that Christ has provided for him.

Key Verse: John 6:63

> The Spirit gives life; the flesh counts for nothing. The words I have spoken to you are spirit and they are life.

1. Who is the source of life?

2. What is the value of the flesh?

3. Where is true life to be found?

4. Where are the words of Jesus to be found?

5. According to John 3:6, can the flesh produce the things of the Spirit?

6. Why then is the new birth in Christ necessary?

The Conflict Between the Spirit and the Flesh

The Conflict Described

Though you are a new creation in Christ, alive spiritually with a totally new identity, there are some things that have not changed. You were born again spiritually, but you were not born again in your **soul** (i.e., mind, emotions, and will) nor your **body.** Therefore there is a conflict between the new you (your living human spirit which is united with the Holy Spirit), and the sin which indwells your still fallen humanity (the flesh).

Paul wrote in Galatians 5:17, "The sinful nature [flesh] desires what is contrary to the Spirit, and the Spirit what is contrary to the sinful nature. They are in conflict with each other, so that you do not do what you want." He went on to describe the results of these two sources in Galatians 5:19-23.

Works of the Flesh

"The acts of the sinful nature are obvious: sexual immorality, impurity and debauchery; idolatry and witchcraft; hatred, discord, jealousy, fits of rage, selfish ambition, dissensions, factions and envy; drunkenness, orgies, and the like."

Fruit of the Spirit

"The fruit of the Spirit is love, joy, peace, patience, kindness, goodness, faithfulness, gentleness and self-control."

(**Note:** Fruit can be defined as an **outward** expression of an **inward** nature.)

The Conflict Illustrated

The programming of the flesh and the Spirit can be described in the form of an AM-FM radio. There is only one radio, and yet there are two distinct bands. An AM station cannot play on the FM channel, and an FM station cannot play on the AM channel.

God is no longer dealing with your old self. He has reckoned it dead at the cross of Christ, and is now only dealing with the **new nature** that He Himself has given to you. On the other hand, Satan cannot touch your spirit, which is sealed by the Holy Spirit of God. He can only continue to appeal to sin in your **flesh**. The programming is set. It is your choice as to which one you will listen to and in which one you will place your faith.

The Root of Sin

Although the visible evidence of sin in a person's life is expressed in many different ways, the root of these sins is always the same—a heart of unbelief. Jesus defined sin in John 16:9 as unbelief in Him.

> They asked Him, "What must we do to do the works God requires?" Jesus answered, "The work of God is this: to believe in the One He has sent" (John 6:28,29).

1. What did the disciples ask Jesus?

2. Have you ever asked the question "What am I supposed to do as a Christian?"

3. What did Jesus say is the "work of God"?

> This is His command: to believe in the name of His Son, Jesus Christ, and to love one another as He commanded us (1 John 3:23).

1. How are the commands of God summarized in the above verse?

   a)

   b)

2. How do these commands compare to what Jesus told His disciples the "work of God is"?

> Whatever is not from faith is sin (Romans 14:23b NKJV).

> Without faith it is impossible to please God (Hebrews 11:6).

3. In light of the above passages, what is essential for pleasing God?

4. What then do you conclude it means to be controlled by your sinful nature?

The New Testament clearly teaches that:

Unbelief = Sin   Faith = Righteousness

Many Christians spend most of their lives attempting to understand their sins in the hope of gaining victory over them. They fail to realize that their sins are merely a **result** of the root sin of **unbelief!** They therefore spend all their time attempting to "cleanse their spiritual lawns" by "ripping off the heads" of all the weeds (sins) rather than dealing with the **root problem** (unbelief), that of not trusting Jesus with every area and situation of their lives.

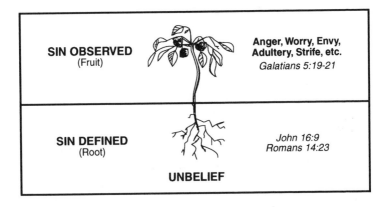

SIN OBSERVED
(Fruit)

Anger, Worry, Envy, Adultery, Strife, etc.
Galatians 5:19-21

SIN DEFINED
(Root)

John 16:9
Romans 14:23

UNBELIEF

Realizing that the root of all sin is unbelief leaves the Christian with only one option: **to turn from his unbelief**

to Christ in faith. He cannot "clean up" his unbelief; he can only begin believing.

God's Solution: Abiding in Christ

Walk in the Spirit

Walk in the Spirit, and you shall not fulfill the lust of the flesh (Galatians 5:16 NKJV).

I am the true vine, and my Father is the gardener. He cuts off every branch in Me that bears no fruit, while every branch that does bear fruit He prunes so that it will be even more fruitful. You are already clean because of the word I have spoken to you. Remain in Me, and I will remain in you. No branch can bear fruit by itself; it must remain in the vine. Neither can you bear fruit unless you remain in Me. I am the vine; you are the branches. If a man remains in Me and I in him, he will bear much fruit; apart from Me you can do nothing. If anyone does not remain in Me, he is like a branch that is thrown away and withers; such branches are picked up, thrown into the fire and burned. If you remain in Me and My words remain in you, ask whatever you wish, and it will be given you. This is to My Father's glory, that you bear much fruit, showing yourselves to be My disciples. As the Father has loved Me, so have I loved you. Now remain in My love. If you obey My commands, you will remain in My love, just as I have obeyed My Father's commands and remain in His love. I have told you this so that My joy may be in you and that your joy may be complete (John 15:1-11).

1. In verse 5, who is the vine?

2. Who is the branch?

3. What is the responsibility of the branch to the vine?

4. What is the responsibility of the vine to the branch?

5. What is the result of the relationship?

6. Does a branch **produce** fruit or **bear** fruit?

7. Can a branch **produce** fruit?

8. How much of the Christian life (fruit) does Christ say you (the branch) can live apart from Him?

9. What is another result of our abiding in Christ (verse 7)?

10. What is the result of our bearing fruit (verse 8)?

Keep Your Eyes on Jesus

Jesus said, "I am the vine." To abide in the vine is to be continually preoccupied with the Lord Jesus Christ—

to search out, meditate upon, and live by faith in what the apostle Paul called "the unfathomable riches of Christ" (Ephesians 3:8).

The Word of God says we are to be continually "fixing our eyes on Jesus, the author and perfecter of our faith, who for the joy set before Him endured the cross, scorning its shame, and sat down at the right hand of the throne of God" (Hebrews 12:2).

Live by Faith in God's Love

Faith says, "As a Christian, I trust my entire acceptance before God upon Christ's completed work on the cross for me."

> He adds: "Their sins and lawless acts I will remember no more." And where these have been forgiven, there is no longer any sacrifice for sin (Hebrews 10:17,18).

1. According to the above verse, is there any provision to be made for sin other than Christ's provision?

2. What should you claim by faith when you do sin (1 John 2:1,2)?

3. In what does God want you to place your faith (1 John 4:16)?

Give Thanks in All Things

> In everything give thanks, for this is the will of God in Christ Jesus for you (1 Thessalonians 5:18 NKJV).

> We know that all things work together for good to those who love God, to those who are the called according to His purpose (Romans 8:28 NKJV).

1. For how many things are you to give thanks?

2. Why?

3. How does giving thanks demonstrate faith?

Live in Total Surrender to God's Will

> I urge you, brothers, in view of God's mercy, to offer your bodies as living sacrifices, holy and pleasing to God—which is your spiritual act of worship. Do not conform any longer to the pattern of this world, but be transformed by the renewing of your mind. Then you will be able to test and approve what God's will is—His good, pleasing and perfect will (Romans 12:1,2).

Because of who you are in Christ, what should you do, according to the above passage?

"_____ your bodies as living sacrifices."

"Be _____ by the renewing of your mind."

Surrender is different from **commitment**. Commitment says, "**I will** do it." Surrender says, "**I can't** do it, Lord, but **You** can."

The idea of surrender can be seen in old World War I movies. Everyone is struggling, fighting, shooting, throwing grenades, and dropping bombs. Suddenly a white flag goes up from one of the trenches. What are these men saying? "I surrender. I don't care what you do to me. I'm sick and tired of being sick and tired." Their future is in the hands of the ones to whom they surrender.

Surrender to God is placing our past, present, and future in His hands and fully **trusting Him with the results.**

Surrender means a willingness to live under the **total authority** of Jesus Christ.

Why not bow your head right now and as an act of your will surrender yourself as a living sacrifice to the Lord? The following is a suggested prayer.

> *Lord Jesus, thank You for giving me Your very own mind and Your own nature to live inside me. Because of the new person You have made me, I now surrender myself as a living sacrifice to You. I know You love me perfectly and I trust You to teach me to walk by faith in Your guidance of my life. Amen.*

Experiencing Freedom in the Spirit

Whenever you are abiding in Christ by faith, you will be walking in the attitude of the spirit expressed in **ACTS** (pages 94-95). However, when the conflict of sin (the outward evidence of unbelief) enters your life, you need to exercise faith in Christ by practicing **RE-ACTS.**

Recognize your sin of unbelief (agree with God concerning your sin).

"When He comes, He will convict the world of guilt in regard to sin and righteousness and judgment: in regard to sin, because men do not believe in Me" (John 16:8,9).

"Everything that does not come from faith is sin" (Romans 14:23b).

Exchange your attitude of unbelief for an attitude of faith in Christ.

"The righteous will live by faith" (Galatians 3:11b).

"Live by the Spirit, and you will not gratify the desires of the sinful nature" (Galatians 5:16).

Abide in the love and grace of Jesus Christ.

"Their sins and lawless acts I will remember no more. And where these have been forgiven, there is no longer any sacrifice for sin" (Hebrews 10:17,18).

"God made Him who had no sin to be sin for us, so that in Him we might become the righteousness of God" (2 Corinthians 5:21).

"I am convinced that neither death nor life, neither angels nor demons, neither the present nor the future, nor any powers, neither height nor depth, nor anything else in all creation, will be able to separate us from the love of God that is in Christ Jesus our Lord" (Romans 8:38,39).

<u>C</u>laim (by faith) your total dependence upon Christ.

> "I am the vine; you are the branches. If a man remains in Me and I in him, he will bear much fruit; apart from Me you can do nothing" (John 15:5).

> "It is God who works in you to will and to act according to His good purpose" (Philippians 2:13).

> "Not that we are competent in ourselves to claim anything for ourselves, but our competence comes from God" (2 Corinthians 3:5).

<u>T</u>hank God in all things.

> "What a wretched man I am! Who will rescue me from this body of death? Thanks be to God—through Jesus Christ our Lord!" (Romans 7:24,25a).

> "Give thanks in all circumstances, for this is God's will for you in Christ Jesus" (1 Thessalonians 5:18).

> "We know that in all things God works for the good of those who love Him, who have been called according to His purpose" (Romans 8:28).

<u>S</u>tand firm in your position in Christ.

> "By one sacrifice He has made perfect forever those who are being made holy" (Hebrews 10:14).

> "Therefore there is now no condemnation for those who are in Christ Jesus" (Romans 8:1).

> "Therefore if anyone is in Christ he is a new creation; the old has gone, the new has come!" (2 Corinthians 5:17).

"It is for freedom that Christ has set us free. Stand firm, then, and do not let yourselves be burdened again by a yoke of slavery" (Galatians 5:1).

10
CHAPTER

Faith, Hope, Love

Throughout the apostle Paul's epistles, you find him commending and encouraging his fellow Christians for their faith, hope, and love (Ephesians 1:15,16; 1 Thessalonians 1:2,3; 2 Thessalonians 1:3,4). The Christian life is lived by faith, encouraged by hope, and exemplified by love. The New Testament points out these qualities as being the evidence to an unbelieving world of a living Lord and a living faith.

Key Verse: 1 Corinthians 13:13

Now abide faith, hope, love, these three; but the greatest of these is love.

1. What are God's priorities for a Christian?

2. What is the greatest of these?

3. How do you see these qualities being interdependent?

Now Abides Faith

The spiritual man has been given the mind of the

Spirit of God so that he might know and understand "the things that have been freely given to us by God" (1 Corinthians 2:12 NKJV), and the power of the Holy Spirit to enable him to live in obedience to the will of God.

1. What work can the Christian do to please God, according to John 6:28,29?

2. What is the will of God, according to John 6:40?

3. How does God sum up His commands to you in 1 John 3:23?

4. According to 1 John 4:4,5, what assures you of victory in everyday life?

5. What do you conclude is God's priority for His children?

Controlled by Faith in Christ

Man's mind under the control of Christ is programmed by God and His Word. His actions are motivated by **faith** in God's commands.

GOD'S WORD

MAN'S ACTIONS CONTROLLED BY FAITH IN CHRIST

Man's mind under the control of Christ is programmed by God and His Word. His actions are motivated by faith in God's commands.

The diagram shows that the mind programmed with _godly thoughts_ from the Word produces _godly actions_ through faith in God and His Word, resulting in _godly emotions._

Faith Is Not a Feeling

Feelings have no intellect. They cannot differentiate between past, present, or future; they are unable to distinguish between reality and fantasy, truth or lies.

For example, a person who pays money, buys a ticket, and enters the theater in order to see a popular horror movie is well aware that there is no real monster in the room. Why then does he feel afraid? Because his **emotions cannot distinguish** between reality and fantasy.

Feelings are never initiators. They merely respond to whatever a person is thinking. Many Christians have adopted the byline of today's generation, "If it feels good, do it!" There is no consistency, however, in a feelings-based experience. If a Christian continually seeks spiritual experiences **apart from the Word of God** he will become fanatical and undisciplined, "having a zeal for God, but not according to knowledge" (Romans 10:2).

Faith, however, is based on **truth,** which never changes. It is interesting to observe that the Bible is almost silent about the subject of feelings, but **obedience by faith** is covered from Genesis to Revelation!

Faith Must Have an Object

1. What is the criterion for scriptural prayer, according to John 15:7?

2. Of what has Christ assured you, according to 1 John 5:14,15?

3. Where do you think the will of God is to be found?

4. Why is it vital for a Christian to be consistently involved with the Word of God?

5. What then is to be the object of the Christian's faith?

Jesus said in John 17:17, "Your word is truth." Therefore the object of the Christian's faith is Christ and His Word. In order to experience the truth of God and His Word, we must not only know what the Word says, but also apply it to our life by acting upon it in faith. Without exercising faith we will become like those mentioned in 2 Timothy 3:7, "always learning and never able to come to the knowledge of the truth" (NKJV).

"Faith is an action taken on the part of man toward a promise made by God."

Now Abides Hope

God not only provided a life of abundance for us here on earth, but also a life of total freedom from sin for all eternity. God has asked us to spend a short period of time here on earth serving Him in the midst of sin in exchange for spending eternity with Him totally free from sin's presence. Jesus told His followers, "In My Father's house are many dwellings; if it were not so, I would have told you. I go to prepare a place for you. And if I go and prepare a place for you, I will come again and receive you to Myself, that where I am, there you may be also" (John 14:2,3 NKJV).

> How great is the love the Father has lavished on us, that we should be called children of God! And that is what we are! The reason the world does not know us is that it did not know Him. Dear friends, now we are children of God, and what we will be has not yet been made known. But we know that when He appears, we shall be like Him, for we shall see Him as He is. Everyone who has this hope in Him purifies himself, just as He is pure (1 John 3:1-3).

1. What is the reason for the Christian's hope (verse 1)?

2. As children of God, what shall we someday become (verse 2)?

3. What is the result when a Christian lives with this hope in his heart (verse 3)?

Since the prophecies concerning Christ's **first coming** have been literally fulfilled, consistency demands that the unfulfilled promises of His **second coming** should also be fulfilled in the very same literal way.

As surely as God's Word is true, one of these days, and it could be **today,** Jesus will come and all who know Him will rise to meet Him in the air. Let those who know Him live in the blessed hope and expectation of our Lord's return.

Our hope of Christ's return should enable us to see life in light of eternity and set our priorities accordingly. It is our paramount motivation for understanding the Lord's words to "seek first His kingdom and His righteousness" (Matthew 6:33). All things we see today will someday vanish; only those things we cannot see will remain forever, "for the things which are seen are temporary, but the things which are not seen are eternal" (2 Corinthians 4:18 NKJV).

The Greatest of These Is Love

God's Love Toward Us

There are two words used in the original language of the New Testament for love, the Greek words **phileo** and **agape.** Simply defined, **phileo** is **friendship** love (e.g. Philadelphia, city of brotherly love, and philanthropic, love of mankind). **Phileo** is a **conditional love** based on the actions, character, or lovability of the object. **Agape,** on the other hand, is **unconditional love**. It is not based upon the character of the one being loved, but on the character of the one expressing love. Agape is God's love, and His love is not determined by whether we are deserving or not, but by the fact that He has chosen to love us unconditionally.

1. How did God demonstrate His love for you, according to John 3:16?

2. What does God want you to both **know** and **believe,** according to 1 John 4:16?

As a Result of God's Love for Us...

Our Love for Each Other

As Jesus was facing imminent arrest and crucifixion, He left this significant command with His disciples: "A new commandment I give to you, that you love one another; as I have loved you, that you also love one another. By this all will know that you are My disciples, if you have love for one another" (John 13:34,35 NKJV).

Loving others is to be the lifestyle of a Christian. This command from our Lord can only be obeyed as a result of your understanding His love for you. Loving others is not to be obeyed in order to obtain righteousness (right standing) with God, but as your reasonable service in response to what God has already done for you. God says to His children, "Love one another as I have loved you" (John 15:12 NKJV).

1. What are we commanded to do?

2. How are we to love?

3. What will all know if we love one another?

> As the Father has loved Me, so have I loved you. Now remain in My love" (John 15:9).

1. How does Christ love us?

2. How great a love do you think the Father has for Christ?

3. How then would you conclude we are to love others (John 15:12,13)?

For additional study, see John 15:17; 17:23; 1 John 4:18.

The measure of the vitality of our Christian life is not in how much Christian activity we are engaged in, but in how we are progressing in learning to love one another. Jesus summed up the Christian life in these words: "You shall love the Lord your God with all your heart, with all your soul, and with all your mind. . . . You shall love your neighbor as yourself" (Matthew 22:37,39).

God's Definition of Love

If I speak in the tongues of men and of angels, but have not love, I am only a resounding gong or a clanging cymbal.

If I have the gift of prophecy and can fathom all mysteries and all knowledge, and if I have a faith that can move mountains, but have not love, I am nothing.

If I give all I possess to the poor and surrender my body to the flames, but have not love, I gain nothing.

Love *is patient, love is kind. It does not envy, it does not boast, it is not proud. It is not rude, it is not self-seeking, it is not easily angered, it keeps no record of wrongs. Love does not delight in evil but rejoices with the truth. It always protects, always trusts, always hopes, always perseveres.*

Love never fails. But where there are prophecies, they will cease; where there are tongues,
they will be stilled; where there is knowledge, it
will pass away.

For we know in part and we prophesy in part,
but when perfection comes, the imperfect disap-
pears.

When I was a child, I talked like a child, I
thought like a child, I reasoned like a child. When
I became a man, I put childish ways behind me.

Now we see but a poor reflection as in a
mirror; then we shall see face to face. Now I know
in part; then I shall know fully, even as I am fully
known.

And now these three remain: faith, hope and
love. But the greatest of these is love.

—1 Corinthians 13:1-13

Dear friends, since God so loved us, we
also ought to love one another. No one has
ever seen God; but if we love one another,
God lives in us and His love is made complete
in us (1 John 4:11,12).

1. What does our love for one another prove to the
world?

2. How is God's love made complete in us?

When God the Holy Spirit comes to live in you, it
means that you now have a new mind (1 Corinthians

2:16), new desires, and a new will, "for it is God who works in you both to will and to do for His good pleasure" (Philippians 2:13 NKJV). God desires to express His love and forgiveness to others through you. If the world in which we live is going to see God's love and forgiveness, it is going to have to see it through each one of us. God has never changed His plan to use His followers to express His love and forgiveness to a lost world.

GOD'S WORD
"As I have loved you, so love one another" *(John 15:12).*

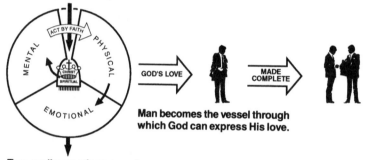

GOD'S LOVE

Man becomes the vessel through which God can express His love.

MADE COMPLETE

True godly emotions are always a result of a mind under the control of the love and grace of God.

Loving by Faith

Faith says, "I believe God will protect me and guide me and remain faithful to me as I am willing to give over my rights to Christ and give myself to others."

God's Command: "A new command I give you: Love one another. As I have loved you, so you must love one another" (John 13:34).

God's Promise: "I can do everything through Him who gives me strength" (Philippians 4:13).

God's Provision: "It is God who works in you to will and to act according to His good purpose" (Philippians 2:13).

God's Protection: "Surely I am with you always, to the very end of the age" (Matthew 28:20b).

The following is a suggested prayer.

> *Father, apart from You I cannot be patient or kind or free from envy and strife, but with You I can do all things. Because You commanded me to love, I know I can trust You to teach me how to love with Your heart, think with Your mind, and see others through Your eyes. Help me, Father, to be filled to the measure with the knowledge of the height, depth, width, and length of Your love for me, and to allow this love to overflow into the lives of others. Amen.*

Remember... Bearing Fruit Is Not a Feeling

God (the vine) wishes to express His love through you (the branch). It is not your responsibility to determine who will benefit from the fruit (love), but only whether you are going to allow God to produce His fruit of love through you.

Complete in Christ

T here are only three priorities in this world that are of any lasting value to God—faith, hope, and love. Without **faith** we cannot please God; without **hope** of His return we cannot find true meaning to the present or purpose for the future; without **loving** others we cannot claim to love God or experience the fullness of His love for us. The Christian life that is characterized by these eternal qualities begins with a mindset—a mind fixed on trusting in Jesus' love and power through every circumstance of life. The Word of God calls this mindset "renewing your mind." As we have stated previously in this book, renewing your mind means seeing things from **God's perspective** rather than from **man's perspective**— to replace doubting with trusting, as an act of the will; to replace negative thoughts with those of hope in a loving and sovereign God; to replace hateful, bitter, indifferent thoughts with those of the fullness of Christ's love for us and others. Any change toward godly behavior, both in actions and reactions, begins with a God-directed **attitude**—a renewing of the mind.

The Christian life is not **difficult** to live—it is

impossible to live! Only Christ can give it and only Christ can live it. Christ's life can only be experienced as we learn to **live by faith** in the One who loved us and gave Himself for us. Begin today to allow Jesus Christ to be Lord of your life every day by voluntarily placing yourself under His authority, and you will begin to see Him conforming your mind, your attitudes, and your life to His own life.

Realizing that sanctification is **God's** work (not yours) will set you free to relax in the security of God's love and grace today and to live free from the anxieties of tomorrow. You can therefore begin accepting yourself and others as God's responsibility and be free to love others as He loves you.

God has provided everything you will ever need to live a joyful, fulfilling, victorious life in Christ—a new nature, a new heart, a new life. Begin today to walk in the reality of these truths. Remember that "you died, and your life is now hidden with Christ in God" (Colossians 3:3). Therefore daily "lay aside" the old self and "put on" the new self that is created in the righteousness of God Himself (Ephesians 4:22-24).

If you have received Jesus Christ through reading this book, or if your life has been impacted in other ways through the ministry of this book, or if you would like more information about our ministry, I would very much appreciate hearing from you. My mailing address is:

Bob George
People to People
2300 Valley View Lane
Suite 200
Dallas, TX 75234

May God bless you with a deep personal understanding and experience of His matchless love and grace!

For every vibrant, fulfilled Christian, there seem to be nine who are "doing all the right things" but still feel bogged down, tied up, or burned out. What is missing?

Classic Christianity
by Bob George

Why do so many Christians start out as enthusiastic believers and end up merely "going through the motions"? Drawing on his own struggles and years of teaching and counseling experience, Bob cuts right to the heart of why Christians sometimes end up disappointed and unfulfilled in their Christian walks.

Have you ever struggled with the questions:

- **What does it mean to have Christ living in me?**

- **How can I experience the joy of the Lord daily?**

- **If I'm a new creation, why do I still struggle with sin?**

In his down-to-earth style, Bob George shows us the answers to these questions *and* the way back to authentic Christianity—the kind that Christ had in mind when He set us free.

Every sincere seeker can get back on track and experience true abundant living. Life's too short to miss the real thing!

In his refreshing bestseller, Classic Christianity, Bob George
pointed the way back to vibrant, life-embracing faith through
the simple and timeless truth of God's grace. Now Growing
in Grace picks up where Classic Christianity left off.

Growing in Grace
by Bob George

The one thing that can keep us from growing in grace is
our age-old preoccupation with self. All around us, people are
fascinated by how they look, how well they are doing, how
much they are accomplishing. It becomes all too easy for this
focus to damage our relationship with Christ.

True growth—growing in grace—is all about keeping our
eyes off ourselves and on Jesus. About believing with utter
certainty that He alone is able to complete His work in us.

In his unique style, Bob shows us that the ability to ride
the storms of life and grow in grace along the way depends not
on our ability to *look* like a Christian, but on our ability to *rest*
like one, knowing we are cared for by a perfect Savior.

Other Books by Bob George

CLASSIC CHRISTIANITY AUDIOBOOK

For believers who want to experience true abundant living but don't have enough hours in their day, the bestselling *Classic Christianity* is now on audiocassettes! Read by Bob George, this abridgement of *Classic Christianity* cuts to the heart of why many enthusiastic Christians end up merely "going through the motions." Rediscover the joy and contentment found in a strong, personal relationship with Christ. (Two cassettes, 180 minutes.)

CLASSIC CHRISTIANITY STUDY GUIDE

Helping tired, disappointed Christians discover the joy of living in grace, Bob's study guide for *Classic Christianity* takes you deep into every subject presented in the book. Space is provided to record thoughts and insights.

CLASSIC CHRISTIANITY ILLUSTRATED

Gifted communicator Bob George combines his most popular contemporary stories and verbal illustrations with easy-to-remember cartoon drawings to help you grasp the life-changing truths of God's Word. These 31 compact stories with matching illustrations cover all the basics, from God's forgiveness to our new identity in Christ. Whether a new Christian or a seasoned believer, concrete visual aids in *Classic Christianity Illustrated* will help you experience the daily joy of letting Christ live His life through *you*.

GROWING IN GRACE STUDY GUIDE

Bob helps Christians live out their freedom in Christ in the face of daily pressures and circumstances. The *Growing in Grace Study Guide* will help you *experience* God's grace as you answer Scripture-based questions and work through your own thoughts and struggles. Discover how to let go of the law, give up forced performance, and grasp the reality of life in Christ.

CLASSIC CHRISTIANITY STUDY SERIES
by *Bob George*

A Closer Look at Faith, Hope, and Love: Bob George explores what faith, hope, and love are and demonstrates how these qualities are active in everyday living. Discover new opportunities for spiritual growth!

A Closer Look at the Finality of the Cross: In the heart of every person is the need to experience forgiveness, be free from guilt, and know God's total acceptance. Discover how Jesus demonstrated the love of God, provided a way for us to experience total forgiveness, and shows us the nature of our new relationship with Him.

A Closer Look at Jesus Christ: With shifting opinions, false teachings, and general confusion in the church, Christians must build their faith on the solid foundation of Jesus Christ. This study explores the facts and examines the claims of Jesus.

A Closer Look at Law and Grace: How does God love and accept us? How are we to live the Christian life? To answer these important questions, this insightful study explores the biblical relationship between law and grace. Understanding their role in your relationship to God will bring joy, freedom, and spontaneity to your life.

A Closer Look at the Truth About Prayer: Can we change God's mind or our circumstances through prayer? If God knows our needs, why should we pray? Is it enough to pray for something once? As Bob shares the keys to effective prayer, you will discover the answers to these questions and more.

A Closer Look at the Reality of the Resurrection: This helpful guide explores the joyous truth that Jesus came not only to die *for* us, but also to restore life *to* us. Discover what "living under grace" means, how you can be led by the Spirit, why being a "brand-new creation" doesn't always feel different, and more.

A Closer Look at the Word of God: Dust off your Bibles and get ready for encouragement! While many people look for answers to life everywhere but the Bible, Bob presents God's Word as the most challenging book of today and brings us to a fresh understanding of the truth and authority of Scripture in *all* circumstances.

A Closer Look at Your Identity in Christ: The issue of identity is central to us. In this exploration, discover the joy and freedom of seeing yourself from God's perspective. Build a self-image based on these life-changing truths: You are loved, forgiven, accepted; God considers you His child; and you are a saint—not a sinner!

Dear Reader:

We would appreciate hearing from you regarding this Harvest House nonfiction book. It will enable us to continue to give you the best in Christian publishing.

1. What most influenced you to purchase *Complete in Christ?*
   - ☐ Author
   - ☐ Subject matter
   - ☐ Backcover copy
   - ☐ Recommendations
   - ☐ Cover/Title
   - ☐ _____

2. Where did you purchase this book?
   - ☐ Christian bookstore
   - ☐ General bookstore
   - ☐ Department store
   - ☐ Grocery store
   - ☐ Other

3. Your overall rating of this book:
   - ☐ Excellent ☐ Very good ☐ Good ☐ Fair ☐ Poor

4. How likely would you be to purchase other books by this author?
   - ☐ Very likely
   - ☐ Somewhat likely
   - ☐ Not very likely
   - ☐ Not at all

5. What types of books most interest you? (check all that apply)
   - ☐ Women's Books
   - ☐ Marriage Books
   - ☐ Current Issues
   - ☐ Christian Living
   - ☐ Bible Studies
   - ☐ Fiction
   - ☐ Biographies
   - ☐ Children's Books
   - ☐ Youth Books
   - ☐ Other _____

6. Please check the box next to your age group.
   - ☐ Under 18
   - ☐ 18-24
   - ☐ 25-34
   - ☐ 35-44
   - ☐ 45-54
   - ☐ 55 and over

Mail to: Editorial Director
Harvest House Publishers
1075 Arrowsmith
Eugene, OR 97402

Name _____

Address _____

City _____ State _____ Zip _____

**Thank you for helping us to help you
in future publications!**